With clear language, engaging stories, words of wisdom from the scholars, and probing questions, David R. Smith strips away any possible confusion about Christianity and brings us right to the heart of our faith. *Christianity. . .It's Like This* gives anyone who wants to follow Jesus a tremendous blueprint. Brand-new disciples and long-term disciple makers will both find great help here.

—Max A. Wilkins
President/CEO, The Mission Society

In a world where young people aren't afraid to ask the big questions, we need to be able to provide big answers. David R. Smith's *Christianity. . .It's Like This* delivers the answers simply, relevantly, and convincingly. . . . His book is an amazing discipleship resource for a searching generation.

—Jonathan McKee
Author of *The Big Deal about Sex*, *Get Your Teenager Talking*, and *The Guy's Guide to God, Girls, and the Phone in Your Pocket*

David was my youth pastor and helped guide me into ministry. He's a legendary communicator, and I'm so glad he's written this book. Now, many others will have access to the Christian faith through easy-to-understand ideas. This book is a must-have for your LifeGroup or Bible study!

—Brian Westlund
Worship Pastor, LifeChurch

It has been my experience for many years that one of the greatest gifts you can give a student is a sweet taste of scripture. *Christianity. . .It's Like This* by David R. Smith is written with the same desire, to have an excellent use of apologetics and sound biblical principles. It also manages to be very devotional. I believe this book will be a great tool for those who want to equip their students to take their lives to the next level.

—Dr. Jay Strack
President and Founder of Student Leadership University

David R. Smith shows the unique and God-given ability to communicate the Gospel and biblical principles in a clear, effective manner. David cuts to the core of who we are as Christians and who we can be through Christ.

—Kerry Klecic
FOX 13 (WTVT)

Having heard David speak many times, I can confidently say he knows how to connect with real people and deliver a message that's both relevant and theologically sound. In the pages of *Christianity. . .It's Like This*, readers will experience David's unique ability to deliver high-concept truths in bite-size pieces.

—Carmen Brown
The Morning Cruise || The JOY FM

This remarkable young pastor has a gift for pointing others to Jesus in accurate, but simple, terms. Sound and straightforward, *Christianity...It's Like This* is a much-needed book that can be used to reach those without faith and help those with it to grow. David has given us an incredible tool, and I strongly recommend we use it.

—Dr. Charles Roesel
Pastor Emeritus, First Baptist Church of Leesburg
Ambassador to the North American Mission Board
Author of *It's a God Thing*

David R. Smith's passion for pointing others to Christ and teaching them God's Word both come through in his latest book. *Christianity...It's Like This* offers pastors, teachers, and church leaders a powerful tool to help others understand biblical truth. Smith's use of gripping stories and simple explanations will help others harness a deeper understanding of God's Word. Do your small groups a favor and get this book!

—Paul Alonso
Senior Pastor, Wahoo Baptist Church

Acknowledging that the language of the church has sometimes proven confusing, David R. Smith develops biblical themes in *Christianity...It's Like This* that anyone can readily comprehend. His ultimate goal is to show how the Gospel can transform lives, but David also issues a challenge to church leaders, reminding us to be sensitive in communicating our world-changing truth.

—Dr. Donald Minshew
Executive Director, Gulf Stream Baptist Association

An *Uncomplicated* Look
at What It Means
to Be a *Christ-Follower*

Christianity...
It's Like This

David R. Smith

SHILOH RUN PRESS

To everyone ascending Mars Hill,
He need not remain unknown.
Acts 17:23

Print ISBN 978-1-63058-689-8

eBook Editions:
Adobe Digital Edition (.epub) 978-1-63409-192-3
Kindle and MobiPocket Edition (.prc) 978-1-63409-193-0

Published by Shiloh Run Press, an imprint of Barbour Publishing, Inc., P.O. Box 719, Uhrichsville, Ohio 44683, www.barbourbooks.com

Our mission is to publish and distribute inspirational products offering exceptional value and biblical encouragement to the masses.

Member of the
Evangelical Christian
Publishers Association

Printed in the United States of America.

Contents

It's Like This. . .

W^e were still drinking our first Cokes at a pizza joint one Sunday night in Miami when Jordan, one of my high school seniors, shook his head in frustration. "I just don't get it. Some of the stuff that guy said confused me. . .and some of it freaked me out!"

"That guy" was a Christian pastor.

Even as a pastor myself, I had thought it was a rather unusual message. The speaker went on and on for almost an hour and used every seventeen-syllable word he knew associated with Christianity. Incarnation. Justification. Sanctification. Reconciliation. *For Jordan, it just led to a lot of perspiration.*

Everything the guy said was important, but the way he *explained* it didn't help Jordan *understand* it. My young friend finally looked at me and asked, "What does it all mean?"

I took a deep breath, and said, "Jordan, it's like this. . ."

Starting at the beginning, and using words Jordan could understand, I walked him back through the speaker's (long) message. When I finished (somewhere in the middle of my third refill), I looked Jordan in the eye and asked him if he finally understood. He said he did and then asked one last question.

"Why didn't the speaker just *say* that?"

To be honest, I didn't know.

Like Jordan, you may have important questions about life and faith that need answering, but you know you can't trust everything you find on a Google search. And books about Christian theology—*average weight, seventy-three pounds*—offer little more than vocabulary training. *Jesus' substitutionary death offers atonement for our transgressions. The hypostatic union of the Incarnation is the most accurate Christology.* Instead of getting answers, you probably just get a headache. It happened to Jordan; it could happen to anyone.

Like the fat grams in the pizza and the sugar calories in the Coke, that conversation stuck with me. Jordan's confusion prompted me to reflect on the simplicity of Jesus' message. When He taught people, He used words, phrases, and ideas that people understood. Take a look for yourself:

- *What is the kingdom of God like? What shall I compare it to? It is like a mustard seed. (Luke 13:18–19)*

- *The kingdom of heaven is like treasure hidden in a field. (Matthew 13:44)*

- *The kingdom of heaven is like a net. (Matthew 13:47)*

Over and over, Jesus employed simple expressions to teach people. Granted, they might not have *liked* what they heard, but they usually *understood* what Jesus said. When Jesus discussed something beyond our understanding—for example, the kingdom of heaven—He began by saying, "It's like this," and then used something from people's daily lives, something they already understood, to make His point.

Brilliant!

Too many Christians do the exact opposite; they use complex expressions to convey simple truths about Jesus.

This book is for every "Jordan" who wants to know more about God, faith, the Bible, or life in general. We'll talk about Christianity "in plain English" because when Jesus spoke, it was in plain English, right? (Okay, *technically*, it was in Aramaic—but it was *plain* Aramaic!)

But plain doesn't mean powerless. A "diluted" version of Christianity won't answer your big questions. So, we'll skip over the tricks and get right to the truth. Every chapter in this book focuses on one key element of Christianity but comes in two parts. The first part discusses the subject in simple—but detailed—terms, offering a mix of everyday examples *and* technical explanations (called Scholar's Sidebars) for those who want it.

The second part of each chapter, called Sessions, offers you the opportunity to explore the subject in greater depth by answering thought-provoking questions about a Bible passage on the topic. In these Sessions, we'll share *even more* illustrations and examples, from the website that led to the creation of this book: www.ItsLikeThis.org. Though the Sessions can be completed individually, I strongly encourage you to work through them with a group of friends. The power of group study leads to personal growth like nothing else in the world.

Some people think Christianity is confusing; some believe it's just a list of mundane rules; and some even dismiss it as an ancient and useless religion. But Christianity isn't any of those things.

It's like this. . .

1

God

What is He like (if He even exists?)

When I think about God, I usually think about aliens. Let me explain.

Even though the 1996 movie *Independence Day*, starring Will Smith, Bill Pullman, Jeff Goldblum, and several other terrific actors, is a little bit old, it's still one of my all-time favorites. The gist of the movie is that aliens invade Earth on July 2, with plans to destroy humanity. By July 4, the date on which America declared its initial independence from England, we must fight for it once again...but this time from aliens.

Oh yeah...it's on!

Granted, Hollywood has made a lot of alien movies, and some have better CGI than *Independence Day*, but when Captain Hiller (Will Smith) opens up the alien spaceship he shot down, punches the alien in the face, and says, "Welcome to Earth!" it's a moment of pure, red-blooded, Grade-A testosterone. Of course, when Captain Wilder (Harry Connick

Jr.) says, "Let's kick the tires and light the fires, big daddy!" I've never wanted to own an F/A-18 Hornet so badly in my life.

Like every other alien movie produced by Hollywood, *Independence Day* revolves around two basic questions:

Do aliens exist?

If so, what are they like?

Every sci-fi flick answers those questions in its own way. Sometimes the aliens are green, sometimes they're red, and sometimes they even look like us. Sometimes the aliens are good and sometimes they're bad. But the same two questions are at the heart of every alien movie.

I think most people ponder the exact same questions about God:

Does He exist?

If so, what is He like?

Now do you see why I think of aliens when I think of God?

Maybe you've never answered those two questions about God. Maybe you've never even gotten to the second question because you doubt the answer to the first one. That's fair. Seriously. After all, these are the two biggest questions in life. But there's a definitive answer for both of those questions.

That Big Spaceship in the Sky

Though I do not believe in the existence of aliens, I should probably go on record and say that I believe in the existence of God. There are lots of good reasons for both beliefs.

First, I can honestly say that I've never seen a flying saucer; I've never been abducted by aliens for weird experiments (like the guy from *Independence Day*); nor have I come across any compelling evidence for their existence. In no way has my life—or anybody's that I know—been affected by visitors from another planet. In fact, I'm much more worried about my home being invaded by termites than Martians.

But when I look at the world around me, at the people who share it with me, and even into the recesses of my own heart, I come to a completely different conclusion about God.

Every single human being who has ever lived has wondered whether or not God is real. I've done it. You've done it. We've all done it. Answering that question is at the center of our existence as humans. Think about it: squirrels aren't concerned about the existence of God, or the next thousand years, or who will win the Super Bowl. They only care about their next acorn. We're the only life form that wonders if there's something—or someone—out there. . . .

Throughout history, billions of people have wondered whether there's a good reason to believe that God exists. My answer is, "No, there's not one good reason to believe God exists. . .there are *lots* of good reasons to believe He exists."

Let's look at some of those reasons and see if, in the process, we can discover what God is like.

Reason #1 for God's Existence: Stuff Exists

Where did trees come from? Or stars? Where did *we* come from?

We might answer that last question by saying, "From our

The Cosmological Argument for the Existence of God

Yes, it's a long name, but that's what this idea is called. Fortunately, the concept is quite basic; it goes like this:

1. If something exists, it had to have a cause.
2. The universe exists.
3. Therefore, the universe had a cause.

That "cause" was God, or what some philosophers call the Prime Mover (or First Mover). If a creation exists, a Creator must also exist.

parents," but then we instantly have another question on our hands: "Well, where did *they* come from?" We'd probably think, "From our grandparents," but then we're faced with the same question all over again: "But where did *they* come from?" If you're patient enough, I suppose you could ask that question all the way back—past George Washington, past Moses, and past Noah—to Adam and Eve. But then, there's one nagging question remaining: "Yeah, but where did Adam and Eve come from?"

The same question applies to everything we see, not just humanity. How did the galaxies come to be? Where did dinosaurs come from? How did we get gravity, light, and energy?

According to many brilliant thinkers, the answer to those questions is *God*.

Think about it like this. A cake has to have a baker, right? Doesn't a building have to have a builder? How about a book? It needs a writer. Likewise, a creation (like our universe) must have a Creator.

Epicurus, an ancient Greek philosopher, summed up our reality like this: "Something obviously exists now, and something never sprang from nothing."

Good point, Epicurus.

Look around the room you're sitting in. See that cup on the table? How did it get there? Didn't someone have to put it there? What about the chair you're sitting in? Somebody had to build it. What about your clothes? *(I trust you're wearing clothes. . . . If you're reading this naked, I insist that you go and put on some pants!)* Didn't someone have to make your clothes?

Of course! Everything that exists in this universe came from something. And lots of people have lots of reasons to believe the "something" is God. And why not? The opening line of the most unique book on the planet says, *"In the beginning, God created the heavens and the earth"* (Genesis 1:1). From before time began, God was hard at work creating life in what we now know as the universe. But it gets even more interesting when we look at the *sort* of universe we live in. . . .

Reason #2 for God's Existence: The Uniqueness of Our Design

Think about these facts for a moment:

- Earth is located in what scientists call "the habitable zone," an orbit that is the perfect distance from the sun to ensure that our planet is neither too hot nor too cold.

- Earth is the only known planet that has water in liquid form.

- Earth has the perfect balance of water and land.

- Earth has an atmosphere that shields its inhabitants from dangerous radiation and (most) of the debris flying through space.

- Earth has one moon—of perfect size and proximity—which ensures life-giving tides for the creatures of the seas.

We could go on and on. We haven't even mentioned the importance of the 23.5° tilt of Earth's axis. In short, it seems obvious that Earth was carefully designed to sustain life.

When you start thinking about it, Earth is pretty special. Scientists stand in awe when looking at the universe, just like any of us would stand in awe when looking at the Great Pyramids or the Taj Mahal or the Golden Gate Bridge. . .or a perfectly crafted double bacon cheeseburger.

It's even more stunning when we think about ourselves. Consider the fact that no two humans have the same exact fingerprint or DNA. Think about how intricate the human eye is or how powerful the human brain is. We carry the trademarks of a wonderful design, and a design calls for a designer, does it not?

The Teleological Argument for the Existence of God

Sometimes, this argument is simply referred to as Design Theory because of the precise design our world seems to have. Telos is the Greek word for "purpose" and hints at the possibility that God had a really important purpose for Earth. . .providing a home for us!

Without a doubt, our planet is completely unique in comparison to the billions of other planets in countless other galaxies floating through space.

As the incredibly intelligent French philosopher Voltaire once said, "If a watch proves the existence of a watchmaker but the universe does not prove the existence of a great Architect, then I consent to be called a fool."

Piggybacking on that thought, William Paley, a Christian who lived and worked during the eighteenth century, put it like this: "If I'm walking through a field and stub my toe on a rock and someone asks me how the rock got there, I'd probably say that it had been there forever. But if I'm walking through the same field and stumble upon a watch, it would be silly to think that it had been there forever. Somebody had to build the watch. In other words, there had to be a watchmaker."

If we were to find an iPhone in a forest, it would be really foolish to think it had been there all along and had no purpose for existing. You'd know that the delicate touchscreen, the powerful computer, the rechargeable battery, and a hundred other brilliant parts were intentionally put together by someone for the purpose of making phone calls. . .*and playing Flappy Bird.* There'd be no doubt in your mind that someone had intricately designed that iPhone.

If we can look at a watch or a smartphone and believe there was a maker, why shouldn't we look at a special creation that includes photosynthesis, gamma bursts, supernovas, and tons of other cool features, and believe there's a special Creator? A fantastic creation must mean there's a fantastic Creator nearby. That seems to be what the prophet Isaiah had in mind:

> *For this is what the* LORD *says—he who created
> the heavens, he is God; he who fashioned and*

made the earth, he founded it; he did not create
it to be empty, but formed it to be inhabited—he
says: "I am the LORD, and there is no other."
(Isaiah 45:18)

These first two reasons only hint at God's *existence.* Let's look at one more reason for His existence that also gives us a few clues as to what He's like.

Reason #3 for God's Existence: The Reality of Good and Evil

You may not know it, but C. S. Lewis, the world-famous author who wrote The Chronicles of Narnia, was actually a devout Christian. But interestingly, he became a Christian after many years as a hard-core atheist. When he finally became a believer, Lewis gave the world one of the best reasons for God's existence, and it goes right back to the rule our moms gave us for playing in the sand box together: *play nice.*

Okay, that's a little bit of an oversimplification, but it does set the right tone. Lewis looked out at the world in which he lived—*which had recently been ravaged by two world wars*—and came to the conclusion that it was cruel and unjust. Millions of innocent people had been murdered, children had been orphaned, and entire families were now extinct. That made it easy for Lewis to believe that God didn't exist.

But then he had a disturbing thought: Where had he gotten the concepts of "cruel" and "unjust"? How did he know a person (or action) was cruel unless he had a loving person (or loving action) to compare it to? In other words, he had to know what a "straight" line looked like to be able to label another line "crooked."

Lewis then realized that he must come to terms with a simple fact: all people have an understanding of right and wrong and the difference between them. For instance, everybody on the planet knows that lying, cheating, stealing, and murdering are wrong (even if they do them). Likewise, everybody also knows that honesty, sharing, helping, and giving are good (even if they don't do them). We humans have an innate understanding of good and evil because God has revealed it to us.

The Moral Argument for the Existence of God

This argument not only points to God's existence but also to His character. The bottom line is simple: if God does not exist, then everything is relative and the concept of right (good) and wrong (evil) does not exist. But because right and wrong exist, God must exist. A perfect God would make sure that His creatures know the difference between good and evil, and He would also want them to choose good instead of evil. The God of the Bible has done this.

Not only did God outline His expectations for our lives in the Ten Commandments, a list of moral standards that even children understand, He actually went a step further and embedded that moral code within us. Through the prophet Jeremiah He said it this way: *"I will put my law in their minds and write it on their hearts. I will be their God, and they will be my people"* (Jeremiah 31:33). This not only reinforces the fact that God exists, but it tells us what kind of God He is. The God of the Bible seems very concerned that His people *know* the difference between good and evil, and He seems equally concerned that His people *choose* good over evil.

So far, God appears to be a highly intelligent Creator who has designed an intricate and properly functioning universe. This shows His fondness for order and purpose. He also seems to be highly interested in His creation—especially in us, who are created in His image—to the point that He would engage us with His words so we might know how to live. This proves He cares about us and is dedicated to character, integrity, and justice.

So much more could be said about God, His existence, and His character, but we'll discover even more about Him in chapters 3 and 4. Let's close this chapter by looking at the Bible's defining attribute of God so we can best know what He's like.

The Bible's Take on God

You may be surprised to learn that the Bible doesn't try to *prove* God's existence. Of course, the Bible has a lot—*I mean a lot!*—to say about God, but nowhere does it try to prove that He exists. That's because, from the very beginning (in Genesis) to the very end (in Revelation), we see God highly involved in the lives of the people He created. Whether He's talking with them, performing miracles for them, teaching them truth, saving them from their sins, or overcoming evil on their behalf, God's presence is *evident*. Most people in the Bible had little difficulty believing that He exists. His existence is assumed!

In fact, according to Psalm 14:1, you'd have to be a fool not to believe it: *"The fool says in his heart, 'There is no God.'"* *Fool* is a strong word, but it's one that God feels fits the bill. After all, a certain amount of mental silliness is required to completely dismiss the rationale for God's existence outlined in the arguments above.

By the Bible's standard, the late Christopher Hitchens, though very well educated, was a fool. During his lifetime, "Hitch" published several books denying the existence of God and the legitimacy of (any) faith. His unique, and somewhat comical, theories—which attracted a large following—dismissed altogether the possibility of an afterlife. Not only did he strike at the core of religion, he sometimes did so in an inflammatory manner. Whether it was one of his columns, articles, speeches, or books, everyone knew which side of the fence Hitch was on when it came to God. In 2007, he even published a book that bore the title of his personal mantra, *God Is Not Great.*

Hitchens did anything he could to convince others of his opinion. In a famous debate at American Jewish University in early 2011, the world-renowned atheist squared off against Sam Harris and rabbis David Wolpe and Bradley Artson on the subject of death and the afterlife. Hitchens jokingly said, "It will happen to all of us, that at some point you'll be tapped on the shoulder and told, not just that the party is over, but slightly worse: the party's going on but you have to leave. And it's going on without you."

The crowd laughed at his clever remark about death, and

he continued with his sarcastic dismissal of God and faith. But his statement reveals some inconsistencies in his views:

Who is it that taps people on the shoulder?

Who gets to say when "the party" is over?

For that matter, who threw the party in the first place?

On December 15, 2011, at the age of sixty-two, Hitch was "tapped on the shoulder" and was given the opportunity to put his theories about God and the afterlife to the test. Though no one knows for sure, it appears as if, from all public accounts, Hitch denied God's existence until the very end. Consequently, he forfeited the love that God had offered him. And that was a huge loss for Hitch, because God's crowning attribute is love.

Describing God can be a daunting task because He has so many wonderful attributes. He's supernatural. He's all-knowing. He's all-powerful. He's all-present. We're none of those things. We have to rely on what the Bible says about God, and fortunately, the Bible describes Him perfectly. . .and *simply*. In one word, no less!

According to 1 John 4:8–10, that word is *love*:

Whoever does not love does not know God, because God is love. This is how God showed his love among us: He sent his one and only Son into the world that we might live through him. This is love: not that we loved God, but that he loved us and sent his Son as an atoning sacrifice for our sins.

God doesn't just *give* love; He *is* love! According to the apostle John, God's love for us is so great that He was willing to give the life of His perfect Son, Jesus, to save us from our sin. (We'll talk more about Jesus in chapter 3.)

Not only does God actually exist, but He is also a God of absolute, perfect love. It doesn't get any better than that! Voltaire once said, "If God did not exist, it would be necessary to invent Him."

Fortunately, God does exist, and He offers us His perfect, life-changing love to prove it.

Session 1

God

What is He like (if He even exists?)

Big Idea: Not only does God exist, but He wants to change our lives with His love.
Passage: Exodus 3:1–15
Discussion Starter: *Moon Landing: The Evidence Left Behind*

In July 1969, the world watched with bated breath as three men left Earth and headed for the moon aboard a Saturn V rocket. On July 20, astronauts Neil Armstrong and Buzz Aldrin landed on the dusty lunar surface and within hours were strolling across the Sea of Tranquility.

But they hadn't traveled a quarter-million miles just to walk around; there was work to be done.

And lots of it!

The two men snapped tons of pictures, snagged soil samples,

and harvested forty-nine pounds of moon rocks. But they didn't just *take* things from the moon; they intentionally *left* some items, as well.

Along with a specially designed American flag, which they planted on the surface of the moon, the two astronauts deployed the Lunar Laser Ranging Retroreflector Array (*try saying that five times fast!*), a large assembly of prisms designed to reflect incoming light back to its source. This device allows scientists on Earth to fire laser beams at the moon and have them bounce directly back to the source, so that the distance between the two celestial bodies can be accurately measured.

Oh, and the LLRRA—a manmade object sitting on the moon's surface—proves that we were there!

In spite of what conspiracy theorists may say, there is proof that humans have gone to the moon. The LLRRA serves as evidence of mankind's interplanetary visit.

Wouldn't it be nice if God left such plain evidence of Himself and His interaction with us? Granted, God hasn't left any retroreflectors down here, but His fingerprints are all over the place, and we can find them...*if we know what to look for*.

Opening Questions

1. How would you feel if you were one of the astronauts who went to the moon, but then heard other people denying your trip and all your work there?

2. Do you think the Lunar Laser Ranging Retroreflector Array proves that astronauts once walked on the moon? Why or why not?

3. Why do you think people struggle to believe God exists? Has He not left enough fingerprints and evidence?

4. How do you think God feels when humans deny His existence or assume wrong things about His character?

5. What are your honest thoughts about God? Do you believe He exists? If so, what's He like?

Bible Passage
Exodus 3:1–15

This story has a disturbing background. God's people, the Israelites, are being held as slaves in Egypt by a corrupt and murderous Pharaoh. Not only did the Egyptian king force the poor Israelites to build his cities, he had also attempted to eliminate their race by throwing every male Israelite baby into the Nile River. The Israelites cried out to God because of their severe oppression, and God heard their plea. In His plan to liberate the Israelites from their Egyptian slave drivers, God (*"the angel of the LORD"*) approached an Israelite shepherd named Moses, who, though he grew up in the house of Pharaoh, was on the run from his own murderous past. Take a listen to their conversation:

> *Now Moses was tending the flock of Jethro his*
> *father-in-law, the priest of Midian, and he led*
> *the flock to the far side of the desert and came to*

Horeb, the mountain of God. There the angel of the L<small>ORD</small> appeared to him in flames of fire from within a bush. Moses saw that though the bush was on fire it did not burn up. So Moses thought, "I will go over and see this strange sight—why the bush does not burn up."

When the L<small>ORD</small> saw that he had gone over to look, God called to him from within the bush, "Moses! Moses!"

And Moses said, "Here I am."

"Do not come any closer," God said. "Take off your sandals, for the place where you are standing is holy ground." Then he said, "I am the God of your father, the God of Abraham, the God of Isaac and the God of Jacob." At this, Moses hid his face, because he was afraid to look at God.

The L<small>ORD</small> said, "I have indeed seen the misery of my people in Egypt. I have heard them crying out because of their slave drivers, and I am concerned about their suffering. So I have come down to rescue them from the hand of the Egyptians and to bring them up out of that land into a good and spacious land, a land flowing with milk and honey—the home of the Canaanites, Hittites, Amorites, Perizzites, Hivites and Jebusites. And now the cry of the Israelites has reached me, and I have seen the way

the Egyptians are oppressing them. So now, go.
I am sending you to Pharaoh to bring my people
the Israelites out of Egypt."

But Moses said to God, "Who am I that I
should go to Pharaoh and bring the Israelites out
of Egypt?"

And God said, "I will be with you. And this
will be the sign to you that it is I who have sent
you: When you have brought the people out of
Egypt, you will worship God on this mountain."

Moses said to God, "Suppose I go to the
Israelites and say to them, 'The God of your
fathers has sent me to you,' and they ask me,
'What is his name?' Then what shall I tell them?"

God said to Moses, "I AM WHO I AM. This is
what you are to say to the Israelites: 'I AM has
sent me to you.'"

God also said to Moses, "Say to the Israelites,
'The LORD, the God of your fathers—the God
of Abraham, the God of Isaac and the God of
Jacob—has sent me to you.' This is my name
forever, the name you shall call me from
generation to generation."

Study Questions

1. According to this passage, what was God about to do,
and why did He approach Moses?

2. What *sign* did God promise to give Moses to prove that He would be with him?

3. After this radical experience, what do you think Moses would say to someone who claimed God didn't exist?

4. In what ways does God reveal His love in this passage?

Deeper Questions

1. According to a December 2013 Harris Interactive Poll, 74 percent of Americans believe in God. Though still a large majority, it's actually a *decrease* from 2009, when 82 percent claimed to believe in God. Why do you think fewer people believe in God today?

2. Do you think the universe is evidence for God's existence? Why or why not?

3. It requires some thinking and close observation, but the passage from Exodus 3 communicates quite a few qualities about God's character. What are some things that can be said about God based on this passage?

4. In what ways did God change Moses' life at the burning bush (and *after*, if you're familiar with the story)?

Application Questions

1. Do you think God wants to change your life? If so, how? If not, why not?

2. In Exodus 3, God calls Moses to take some radical steps. Based on this study of God and His character, what is one step He's calling *you* to take this week?

Final Word

Maybe this discussion has been life-changing for you. Perhaps you began this session believing that God doesn't exist, but you've come face-to-face with some fairly compelling evidence that He not only exists but also that He loves you perfectly. If that's the case, I want you to know you're not the first person whose mind and heart has been changed by God.

In the story we just read, God deeply changed Moses' life. When we met Moses, he was a murderer on the run who had been forced to tend sheep for many years in the middle of nowhere. But God called him by name, revealed Himself to him in a supernatural way, gave him a tremendous purpose and calling in life to free the nation of Israel from slavery, and filled him with a power that we can only try to imagine. Yeah, it's fair to say that God radically changed Moses' life!

But Moses' life was far from the first—*or last*—life that God has changed. If you look across history, you will see many, many examples of people who've had their lives completely altered by God's love for them. Here are just a few examples of men and women who had a life-changing encounter with a real and loving God:

- *Paul.* Originally named Saul, he was a member of the Pharisees (the group partly responsible for Jesus' death). He consented to the murder of Stephen, the first person to die for being a Christian, and he persecuted many other believers in ancient Israel. In other words, he was working against God. But one day as he traveled to Damascus to arrest Christians, he encountered God's Son, Jesus, and his entire life was changed. He became a Christian, preached the Gospel, planted churches, traveled on several missionary trips, and wrote a large portion of the New Testament. He was eventually beheaded for being a Christian. *There's no doubt Paul believed God was real; no one dies for a lie.*

- *William Wilberforce.* Born into a wealthy family, Wilberforce took full advantage of his family's money. He selfishly enjoyed almost every vice of his day and barely applied himself in school. He became a member of Parliament in 1780 at the young age of twenty-one, but in 1784, God radically changed his life. Beginning in 1787 and continuing for the next forty-six years, Wilberforce worked tirelessly to end slavery in the British Empire. On July 26, 1833, a mere three days before his death, the Slavery Abolition Act was passed, bringing to an end the cruel practice of slavery in the British Empire. Just as God had done with Moses, He plucked William Wilberforce's mediocre life from the pages of history and used him to rescue millions of people from slavery. *Through Wilberforce, the real God made a real difference in our world.*

- *Lottie Moon.* She was named Charlotte Digges Moon at birth, but everyone called her Lottie. Her wealthy family lived in Virginia, and Lottie was given the nicer things in life. Though raised by staunch Baptists, Lottie was a bit unruly, and even mischievous, during childhood. However, in 1858, at the age of eighteen, she experienced a spiritual renewal after meeting God while listening to an evangelist talk about missions. She then spent almost forty years as a missionary in China, leading people to Christ, starting schools, and promoting future missionary work. Today a global offering collected in her name ensures that entire unreached communities will receive God's life-giving words. *Her changed life changed millions of other lives, as well.*

- *Chuck Colson.* He was a successful lawyer, who worked for President Nixon...until he was sent to prison for participating in the infamous Watergate scandal. After the high-profile crime, Colson became a born-again Christian when he realized there was a God who loved him even though he suffered the shame of an entire nation. Upon his release, he founded Prison Fellowship, a ministry that has led thousands of inmates to faith in Christ. Prison Fellowship also helps take care of the families of incarcerated men and women; the Angel Tree project delivers millions of gifts each Christmas to boys and girls whose parents are in prison. *God changed Chuck Colson's life behind bars and then set him free to change lives across the nation.*

These are just a *few* of the men and women who have had their lives radically changed by God. If you could ask them, they'd tell you they had no doubt that God existed and that His love was great. They saw the evidence of His work, they noticed His fingerprints all around them, and they allowed God to change them into completely different people.

Even though God has changed many, many lives, He wants to change at least one more—*yours.* He wants you to know He's real and He wants to change your life with His love.

Will you let Him?

2

The Bible

Can it really be trusted?

Sometime during the early morning hours of May 12, 1967, several buildings at First United Methodist Church in Lake City, Florida, caught on fire. For seven long hours, the flames tortured and destroyed the historic downtown structures. When the smoke finally cleared, grieving church members took stock of all they'd lost.

And, ironically, what they'd gained.

When the sun finally rose on that terrible morning, daylight revealed what little was left. The chapel was nothing more than a pile of ashes. The children's educational building was a smoldering heap of charred debris. The beautiful sanctuary had completely collapsed, not a single wall was left standing, and the roof had been completely consumed by the flames. Most of the sanctuary's furnishings were totally destroyed or unrecognizable; microphone stands were now fused pieces of twisted metal, the pews had been reduced to small chunks of smoking wood, and the oak pulpit was nothing but a heap of gray embers.

But remarkably—*miraculously*—the Bible that had rested on the pulpit was not destroyed as one would expect, given its highly flammable pages. Granted, the leather cover that enclosed the Bible was ruined, but most of the pages of Scripture were largely unharmed. When first responders were finally able to retrieve the Bible, they found it opened to the book of Job, a well-known story of harrowing loss and tremendous suffering that eventually ends in restoration and great blessing.

Upon reflection, it's easy to see the correlation between the church's experience and the experiences of Job. Both lost a great deal; but in the end, both reveled in the truth of God's words. After all, it was Jesus who said, *"Heaven and earth will pass away, but my words will never pass away"* (Mark 13:31).

The point here is not that Bibles aren't flammable; they're made of paper, and across the years, many have *intentionally* been burned. But this event served as a remarkable reminder to the people of Lake City First United Methodist Church about the power and promise behind God's words. That scorched Bible is now enclosed by glass and on display in their new church building, testifying to the truth of Scripture.

A One-of-a-Kind Book

This book is about Christianity, so we must talk about Christianity's book, the Bible. The Bible is often referred to as "The Book" or "The Good Book," but actually, the Bible is a book made up of many books.

Sixty-six to be exact.

The Old Testament (Genesis to Malachi) consists of thirty-nine books. Many of these are fairly long and record the ancient history of God's interaction with people. For instance, the stories of Adam, Noah, Abraham, Moses, Samson, David, Jonah, and many others are told in the Old Testament.

The New Testament (Matthew to Revelation) has twenty-seven books. Most of these are fairly short, and in one way or another focus on just one story: Jesus, the Son of God, coming to earth as a man. Four of these books (Matthew, Mark, Luke, and John), are biographies of Jesus that we call the Gospels, which means *good news.* They record His birth, life, death, and—most importantly—His resurrection; they also recount Jesus' many miracles, parables, and teachings. Good News *indeed.*

Throughout the Old and New Testaments, almost every form of writing is represented. For example, the books of Genesis and Acts contain a lot of history. Books such as Leviticus and Deuteronomy contain hundreds of laws. The poetic book of Psalms is essentially the Bible's iTunes; it has 150 songs in it. Books like Isaiah, Obadiah, and Zephaniah record tons of prophecies (some that have already been fulfilled, and some that are yet to be fulfilled). The Song of Solomon is a book filled with romantic verse. All in all, the Bible is a well-rounded piece of literature that contains many different kinds of writings.

It's pretty cool, but that's not what makes the Bible a one-of-a-kind book.

David R. Smith

Building the Book

How the Bible became one book is a miraculous story in itself. Though most books have just one author, the Bible has about forty. These were fascinating people, chosen by God, who came from all walks of life. Some were kings and some were military leaders. Others were tax collectors, fishermen, or musicians. There was even a doctor and a couple of shepherds who helped to write the Bible.

If you think that's interesting, it gets better.

These people didn't even speak the same language...mainly because they didn't all live on the same continent. That's right; some of the writing took place in Africa, some happened in Asia, and some in Europe.

The Bible, written on three continents, was originally recorded in three different languages, as well. Most of the Old Testament was written in Hebrew, and most of the New Testament was written in Greek. But there are a few lines here and there in both testaments that were written in Aramaic.

That's really cool, too. But it's still not what makes the Bible one of a kind.

Autographs

The actual scrolls written on by the actual hand of Moses (and the actual scrolls written on by the actual hands of Micah, Malachi, and Matthew, etc.) are called "autographs". The Bible's autographs were the original writings of God's words. Unfortunately, every single autograph has been lost over the course of history, but we don't need to worry. Those originals were copied hundreds—and sometimes, thousands—of times. In fact, the Bible was the most-copied and most-circulated writing in ancient times; archaeologists have found almost twenty-five thousand pieces of the New Testament alone!

The Bible wasn't written all in one year. It wasn't even written during a single decade or century. In fact, it wasn't written during a single millennium either. The first parts of the Bible were written around 1500 BC, and the last parts were written around AD 100. That means it was written over a period of almost 1,600 years.

Fascinating, huh? I bet you think *that's* what makes the Bible one of a kind.

But it's not.

Nope. Just because the Bible was written by roughly forty different people, on three different continents, using three different languages, over the course of sixteen centuries doesn't make the Bible one of a kind. In fact, just because that same Bible has one pure, consistent message about God isn't what makes it one of a kind either.

So, what makes the Bible so unique?

The Bible's Claim to Fame

The Bible is a one-of-a-kind book because it's the only book in the universe that records the actual words of God. Think about that for a moment. That means there is a God... and He has spoken to us! How do we know that? Well, several ways, actually.

For starters, many times in the Old Testament—hundreds of times, in fact—the Bible says, "This is what the Lord says..." Here are just a few examples:

- *This is what the LORD says—Israel's King and Redeemer, the LORD Almighty: "I am the first and I am the last;*

apart from me there is no God." (Isaiah 44:6)

- *This is what the LORD Almighty, the God of Israel, says: "Reform your ways and your actions, and I will let you live in this place." (Jeremiah 7:3)*

- *Therefore say to the people of Israel, "This is what the Sovereign LORD says: 'Repent! Turn from your idols and renounce all your detestable practices!'" (Ezekiel 14:6)*

Another way we can know that the Bible is the word of God is because it records multiple conversations that God had with people just like you and me. There were many, but some of the more famous conversations include the talk He had with Abraham concerning the destruction of the wicked city of Sodom (Genesis 18); the instructions He gave to Moses at the burning bush (Exodus 3); and the conversation he had with Job when Job complained against Him (Job 38–41).

But God didn't just have conversations with people in the Old Testament; He had talks with people in the New Testament, too. If you want proof, just look at the life of Jesus, God's perfect Son. He preached to a huge crowd on the side of a mountain in His famous Sermon on the Mount (Matthew 5–7). He was known to chat it up with sinners...in the homes of lepers (Mark 14). Jesus would talk with people at the drop of a hat...even if the person was in a tree (Luke 19) or interrupting Him in the middle of the night (John 3).

Putting it all together, it looks as if God has a lot to say to us.

That's the point of the Bible: *it is God's communication to us.*

There's one more really good reason to believe the Bible is God's Word: *the Bible itself says it is.* Take a look at 2 Timothy 3:16–17:

> *All Scripture is God-breathed and is useful for teaching, rebuking, correcting and training in righteousness, so that the servant of God may be thoroughly equipped for every good work.*

Scripture—another word for the Bible—has been *breathed out* by God Himself. Because the Bible is the *revelation* of God, we can recognize Him even though we cannot see Him. Aren't we able to recognize our friends and family members by their voices, even if we cannot see them due to a crowd or distance? Likewise, because the Bible reveals God perfectly, we can recognize Him in its words, as well. But the Bible doesn't just reveal the person of God; it reveals His ways, His love, His expectations, and so much more.

No other book on the planet can make that claim. Only the Bible gives us the actual words of God. That's what makes it truly one of a kind.

So What?

If we're honest, we might still say, "So what? So what if the Bible is God's communication to us? Can God's words really be trusted? Does the Bible really tell us the truth? Is the Bible any better than other religious books?"

I get it. We've only got one life to live; should we really base it on the Bible?

Well, if we turn to the Bible to find out about God—which is the best resource available—we see that the Bible describes Him as *love* (1 John 4:8); willing to forgive our sins (1 John 1:9); and compassionate, gracious, patient, loving, and faithful (Psalm 86:15). In other words, the Bible shows God as somebody who loves us desperately. So desperately, in fact, that He sent His Son, Jesus, to pay the price for our sins.

So, if God is perfect, why wouldn't His words be perfect, too?

Because God is truly perfect, He cannot lie; He can only tell the truth. And because He has spoken to us, we can safely assume that what He has said in the Bible is true. Perhaps you've heard the Bible described as inerrant. Well, that word simply means *without error*.

There are plenty of technical definitions of *inerrancy*. Most of them can be a little confusing, so let me give you my definition in plain language: *inerrancy means that everything in the Bible is completely true and can be fully trusted.*

Everything can be trusted? But what about the mistakes in the Bible?

I hear that objection *all the time.* More often than not, it comes from people who genuinely want to believe that God is real and that the Bible is true, but they've listened to skeptics and haters for

Inerrancy

Inerrancy is the belief that, when all the facts about the Bible's original writings (autographs) are known—and interpreted correctly—the Bible will be proved true in all that it claims, whether in reference to doctrine, history, science, society, or the world.

too long. It's hard for them to wrap their minds around the miraculous stories, such as the fall of Jericho's walls.

According to the Bible (in Joshua 6), God told His people to march around the powerful city in a certain manner, then blow their trumpets and give a big shout. . .and the impressive walls of Jericho would come tumbling down before them. According to the Bible, that's exactly what happened.

For a long time, archaeologists were suspicious about the *existence* of Jericho, let alone the biblical story of the walls spontaneously falling down. But in 1997, Dr. Bryant Wood discovered the ancient city of Jericho, and upon excavation of the site, easily determined that the walls of Jericho had *fallen outward*. If the walls had been attacked in the typical way, with battering rams and other siege equipment, they would have been pushed in from the outside. But that's not what happened. In this situation—and all others that it describes—the Bible accurately records history.

Okay, but what about the contradictions in the Bible?

Actually, there *are* some passages in the Bible that seem to contradict one another. But don't be alarmed; even a brief study reveals that the Bible *never* contradicts itself. Here's a great example of one of those instances:

- *Know that a person is not justified by the works of the law, but by faith in Jesus Christ. (Galatians 2:16)*

- *You see that a person is considered righteous by what they do and not by faith alone. (James 2:24)*

On the surface, this sounds very alarming. *(The Bible doesn't have a consistent message on how we are justified! Which one is correct? I really need to know!)*

Actually, *both* are correct. They don't contradict each other because they aren't even talking about the same thing. Yes, in Galatians, Paul was talking about how we are justified—that is, *made right*—with God; he said we are justified through Jesus alone. But James was referring to how we are justified with *other people*. James (rightly) said that we are justified with others by what we do and how we live. It's true; all people—including you and me—want to know if a person can walk the walk and not just talk the talk. All it takes to understand the difference is a simple study of *context*. When we truly study the Bible, we see that it never contradicts itself. *Ever.*

The Bible is the *perfect* collection of God's *perfect* words. That means the Bible is without error and can be trusted fully. Jesus, God's perfect Son, fully believed that His Father's words could be trusted. In John 17:17, Jesus prayed to His Father about His disciples, *"Sanctify them by the truth; your word is truth."*

Do you know how much Jesus believed this? He believed it enough to stake His life on it. The night Jesus prayed this prayer was His last night on earth. He knew that the next day he would die an excruciating death on a cross. If Jesus had any doubt about the truthfulness of God's words, surely He would've bailed out in that desperate moment with His life on the line.

But Jesus didn't jump ship. He knew His Father's words were true, and He continued to base His life on them.

And so should we.

Here's a quick history lesson to further cement the validity of God's words. The ancient church leaders who were responsible for determining which books made it into the Bible— and which books didn't— asked themselves several key questions about each book.

Canon

When you hear the word canon, you probably think about the huge guns on the sides of a pirate ship, like the *Black Pearl*. But those are cannons, with two n's. The word canon, when applied to the Bible, refers to a rule or standard. The books that are in the Bible have all met the standards for inclusion; those that didn't measure up were cut.

Question #1: Was the book written by a spokesman of God?

Moses, who wrote large portions of the Old Testament, talked with God face-to-face. He then took what he'd heard from God and repeated it to God's people. Jeremiah was a well-known prophet in the Old Testament; the book that bears his name includes many references to *"the word of the LORD"* in some form. Here are three quick examples:

- *The word of the LORD came to [Jeremiah] in the thirteenth year of the reign of Josiah. (Jeremiah 1:2)*

- *This is the word that came to Jeremiah from the LORD. (Jeremiah 7:1)*

- *This is what the LORD says. (Jeremiah 17:5)*

Of course, Jeremiah isn't the only example. The four Gospels record the words of God's Son, Jesus; in many cases, those writers were standing next to Jesus when He spoke.

Question #2: Did that spokesperson have God's power in his life?

Let's face it: Anybody can claim to be "sent by God" to "share the words of God." But we should only listen to those people who have the "power of God" evident in their lives. Did Moses have that kind of power? Well, through Moses, God turned the Nile River to blood (Exodus 7). God *literally* parted the Red Sea for Moses (Exodus 14). God even sent food and water into the desert so Moses could feed hundreds of thousands of people every day (Exodus 16–17). There was much, much more, but I'd say that's enough to qualify Moses as God's spokesperson. Thus, the things he heard from God and wrote down were considered to be the words of God. The same is true for the rest of the Bible's writers. Paul, who wrote much of the New Testament, was known for healing the sick (Acts 19) and even raising the dead (Acts 20).

Question #3: Were the writings about God true?

The books and letters and songs that eventually became the Bible were written in multiple languages on multiple continents throughout multiple centuries...but they have only one view of God. If a writer's perspective didn't agree with what was known to be true about God, then that writing was tossed aside. There is only one truth about God, so anything that presented a different (untrue) message had to be cut. *From start to finish, the Bible tells one consistent, true message about God and His mighty love for us.*

Question #4: Was the writing about God accepted by the people of God?

This is where the rubber meets the road. If God's people were told, "These are God's words, so live by them," and they did and were blessed as a result, they took note of that and thought, *Hey, this message truly is from God because it changed our lives.* But if someone said, "This is the message God gave me, so live by it," but it led people away from God, then the people simply dismissed that message. The same still works for you and me today. If we're willing to live by God's words, our lives cannot stay the same.

If they could answer these simple (but very important) questions with a *yes*, then the writing was included in the Bible. The final version of the Bible as we have it today was first introduced in the city of Hippo Regius in North Africa in AD 393. Those ancient church leaders "closed the canon," meaning, they decided once and for all what would be included in the Bible. It's important to note, however, that this decision

Authority

The Bible works because it's true. Since it's true, it serves as the authority in our lives. We obey those who have true authority over us (such as parents, teachers, bosses, or judges), especially if they love us and want the best for us. The Bible's authoritative message reveals God's tremendous love for us and His awesome plan for our lives. That's why we say the Bible has authority.

by these ancient church leaders' didn't *make* the Bible true; their decision simply *recognized* the Bible as truth. In other words, the Bible was God's Word when it was first *spoken* to us by God centuries earlier, not when it was *agreed upon* centuries later.

For thousands of years now, God's words have led millions of people *truthfully* and *accurately*. In short, the Bible *worked* for them; it will *work* for you and me, as well.

But only if we live by it.

In the late nineteenth century, two Russian peasants learned that lesson the hard way. They dutifully taught God's words to their young son, laboring diligently and hoping the Scriptures would shape his life. But sadly, when young Nikita became a man, the Bible had *zero* effect on his life.

Unfortunately for millions of others, Nikita's life would greatly affect their lives.

Without a doubt, Nikita Khrushchev knew God's words. It has been widely reported that Khrushchev memorized *all four Gospels* during his childhood. Once, during a speech in France in 1960, he even claimed to have been a "model pupil" in religion. Late in life, he recalled, "My mother was very religious. Likewise her father—my grandfather. . .I remember being taught to kneel and pray." But because Khrushchev did not live by God's words, those words had no beneficial effect on his life, his attitudes, or his actions.

In fact, as the leader of the Soviet Union, he tried to destroy the very faith he was taught as a child.

Khrushchev prided himself on the scorn he had for religious matters. During murderous "show trials," he gave his unwavering support to political bloodshed. He regularly met his "arrest quotas" and personally signed the death sentences for thousands of Russians, many of whom had been his close friends. Under his leadership, a large percentage of churches were destroyed or closed, and many pastors were arrested and imprisoned (or killed).

In the end, it didn't matter that Khrushchev had been a "model pupil" in religion, or that he had large portions of the Bible memorized. He died a militant atheist, never allowing God's words to truly affect his life.

God's words *must* be applied in our lives. If we're willing to take that risk, we'll see time and time again that the Bible really can be trusted.

Session 2

The Bible

Can it really be trusted?

Big Idea: The Bible contains God's words to us, and it can be completely trusted because all of it is true.
Passage: Psalm 119:89–96
Discussion Starter: *Battlefield Miracle: Bible Stops Bullet*

The Bible is a one-of-a-kind book. Just ask Private First Class Brendan Schweigart; he'll tell you. Of course, PFC Schweigart may be a little biased. After all, the Bible literally saved his life.

While on patrol in Iraq in August 2007, PFC Schweigart was hit by a sniper's bullet. But instead of killing the young Marine, the bullet lodged in the Bible he carried in his uniform's chest pocket.

It should probably be stated that Bible-stops-bullet stories have been around for at least two hundred years. In fact, the tales are so well known that the possibility of such a feat was actually put to the test on the hit TV show *MythBusters*. (By the way, on that episode, it was "scientifically proven" that a Bible could *not* stop a small caliber bullet, let alone the high-powered bullets used in warfare today.)

Maybe their calculations didn't account for God's will. . . .

Here's what happened. During a recovery mission in Baghdad, PFC Schweigart was struck by a sniper's bullet in his side. The bullet entered his body under his arm, a place his military-issued bulletproof jacket didn't cover. The round then exited through his chest, where it lodged in the pages of the Bible the young soldier carried under his bulletproof chest shield.

Granted, the body armor worn by today's military personnel does a good job of keeping bullets *out*, but on the occasion that a bullet happens to find its way *in*, the gear also does a good job *keeping* the bullet in, allowing it to ricochet back into the person's body and possibly causing massive damage to vital organs. Schweigart is convinced that had the bullet hit the inside of his chest plate, it probably would have killed him. But instead of the bullet bouncing off the hard plate, it was trapped in the soft pages of his Bible.

That's why Brendan Schweigart believes the Bible is a one-of-a-kind book.

Now, you may be thinking, "Yeah, yeah. A lot of books might have stopped that bullet. *War and Peace* is thick enough. My algebra book is definitely thick enough! Heck, a stack of twenty or thirty comic books might even be thick enough to do the trick!"

But its bullet-stopping power isn't what makes the Bible a one-of-a-kind book.

Opening Questions

1. How would you feel about the Bible if it had stopped a bullet headed for you?

2. How do you think most people feel about the Bible these days? Why is that?

3. Be honest: Do you think the Bible can be trusted? Why or why not?

Bible Passage

Psalm 119:89–96

> *Your word, LORD, is eternal; it stands firm in the heavens. Your faithfulness continues through all generations; you established the earth, and it endures. Your laws endure to this day, for all things serve you. If your law had not been my delight, I would have perished in my affliction. I will never forget your precepts, for by them you have preserved my life. Save me, for I am yours; I have sought out your precepts. The wicked are waiting to destroy me, but I will ponder your statutes. To all perfection I see a limit; but your commands are boundless.*

Study Questions

1. What are some of the ways the psalmist describes God's words in this passage?

2. In what ways does the writer say that God's words saved his life?

3. What does the psalmist mean when he says he "sought out [God's] precepts" and "will ponder [God's] statutes"?

Deeper Questions

1. The Bible was written by approximately forty different authors from various walks of life, in three different languages, on three different continents, across a time span of 1,600 years, and yet it has one perfectly consistent message: God loves us so much He sent His Son Jesus to rescue us from our sin. In what ways can that give us confidence in the reliability of God's words?

2. Ancient scholars who helped put the Bible together used a strict code of questions when choosing which writings were ultimately from God and which writings weren't. They asked questions such as, "Were the writings from a person who knew and loved God?" and "Did that person have the miraculous power of God in his life?" and "Did the writings teach the perfect truth about God?" and "Were the writings used by God's people in ways that

pleased God?" plus many more. How can this fact give us even more assurance that the Bible really is God's words, which can be fully trusted?

3. Use your smartphone to take a look at the historical teachings of "Listen Up, Tyre!" (http://itslikethis.org/?p=3650) and "Whatever Happened to Assyria?" (http://itslikethis.org/?p=3452). Since God's words have been so accurate in the past, does it help you to trust His words for your future? Why or why not?

4. Let's look at two different passages, one about gossip and one about selfishness. (Bear in mind that both were written several thousand years ago.)

- *A perverse man stirs up conflict, and a gossip separates close friends. (Proverbs 16:28)*

- *For where you have envy and selfish ambition, there you find disorder and every evil practice. (James 3:16)*

Have you ever seen gossip separate close friends or seen selfish ambition lead to disorder and evil? If so, what does that tell you about the Bible's reliability in our world today?

Application Questions

1. What does God want us to do with His words? How do you know?

2. How would your life be different if you lived according to God's words?

3. What is one change you can make in your life this week to be more in line with God's words?

Final Word

After our discussion about God's words, you may be asking yourself, "So what should I do with the Bible?" The short answer is study it so you can *understand it* and *live by it*.

But because the Bible is a one-of-a-kind book, it reads a little differently from other books. Unlike other books that make you start on page 1 and read straight through to the end, the Bible can safely be read from the beginning, middle, or end. Here are just a few tips to help you get the most out of your study of God's Word.

1. Get a Bible translation you're comfortable with and can easily understand. You and I don't talk in *thees* and *thous*, so it may be best to get a translation of the Bible that uses our modern language.

2. Carve out a part of each day to study the Bible; use a machete if necessary. Let me warn you: if you only study the Bible when you can "find the time," you'll never study the Bible. We don't have loads of free time on our hands. Between school or jobs, homework, sports, chores, and walking the dog, most of us don't have any time left over to study the Bible. To change that, kindly ask your family and your friends to leave you alone for fifteen to thirty minutes each day (during whatever time of the day or night you decide works best) and lock yourself away with your Bible, a small notebook, and a pen. Turn off the TV, shut down the laptop, set aside the smartphone, and remove the earbuds from your ears. If you want to hear from God, you must put yourself in an environment where that's possible.

3. Pray before you start. In fact, pray before you even open the Bible. Ask God to help you understand what you'll read *so you can put it into practice.* There are parts of the Bible that are straightforward and easy to understand, like Exodus 20:13: *"You shall not murder."* But there are also parts of the Bible that are very confusing and difficult to understand, like John 6:53: *"Unless you eat the flesh of the Son of Man and drink his blood, you have no life in you."* Because the Bible contains God's words to us, God understands them better than anyone else. We might as well ask Him for help in understanding His intended meaning.

4. Write down what you learn. . .and what you don't understand. God will always speak to us if we ask Him to. *Why wouldn't He?* Jesus has already died on the cross to save us, so why would God let us wander around without any direction? *He wouldn't!* He'll speak to you and give you direction. And when He does, I strongly suggest that you write it down. Think about it: the God of the universe just spoke to you! Take twenty seconds and write down what He said; also, jot down questions you have that aren't easily answered. It's also very helpful to write down what you're praying about; that will give you an opportunity at the end of each week, month, or year, to reflect on all God has done for you.

5. Last, but far from least, don't let your Bible study time become a stale ritual. If you're studying the Bible out of obligation, not only will you not enjoy it, but you won't get much out of it, either. Think about it this way: If you were able to spend half an hour each day with your favorite person, wouldn't you think ahead about what you're going to talk about? Wouldn't you give some thought to all the pieces of life you want to discuss? Of course you would! So do the same in your relationship with God. Keep it fresh and keep it real.

If you use these simple tips, you'll quickly see why the Bible is a one-of-a-kind book; you'll see that it's the actual words of God for our lives.

The Bible may not tell us everything we *want* to know, but it does tell us everything we *need* to know. For instance, the Bible doesn't tell us if aliens actually exist, what happened to the dinosaurs, or why the Cubs can't win a World Series. But what we *have* discovered from the Bible is far more important than those pieces of trivial information. Because of the Bible, we know who God is and how much He loves us.

That's reason enough to study His words and live by them.

3

Jesus

What makes Him so special?

There's nothing quite like the Great Wall of China. Sure, there are other "fences" in the world. . .*but can they be seen from outer space?* The longest man-made structure in the world draws millions of tourists every year because there's just something special about that particular wall.

There's nothing like the Eiffel Tower either. The instantly recognizable edifice reaches almost one thousand feet into the sky and is illuminated by so many lights that the iron structure looks like a golden spear pointed at the heavens. Even though the awe-inspiring design has been replicated in many other places (including several in the United States), none is as special as the original standing in the center of Paris.

While we're at it, there's also nothing quite like the Grand Canyon. Yeah, it's a big "ditch," but this ditch is thousands of feet deep, an average of ten miles wide rim to rim, and millions of years old! Every year, visitors from around the world stand on its perimeter and gawk at the brilliant colors and magnificent landscape. It may be a ditch. . .*but it still makes us gawk at its beauty*!

Speaking of special, Jesus is extraordinarily unique. Across the pages of history, there has never been anyone like Him, and no matter how long humanity endures, there will never be another like Him.

Ever.

Unfortunately, many people are confused about what makes Jesus special. For example, some think He is special simply because while on earth He was a great teacher. Without a doubt, He was a fantastic teacher—the finest the world has ever seen, in fact. But there have been other great teachers in the past, such as Aristotle and Socrates.

Others think Jesus is special because He has lots of followers. In a social media world focused on amassing followers on Twitter, it's easy to understand why people would think that makes Jesus special; He *does have* a huge number of dedicated followers. But any number of Hollywood actors have lots of followers; even mass murders like David Koresh and Jim Jones can get people to follow them.

Of course, there are some who think Jesus is unique because He is a miracle worker. But there had been other miracle workers before Jesus; they're even mentioned in the Bible alongside Him.

Yes, Jesus is a great teacher, a great leader, and a miracle worker, but there have been other great teachers, great leaders, and miracle workers in our world. For Jesus to be completely unique, He needs to possess attributes that no one else can rightly claim. For Jesus to truly stand out, there must be aspects of His life that make Him stand alone.

The Bible, which we've already seen is a one-of-a-kind book that can be completely trusted, shows that Jesus *does* possess those kinds of attributes that set Him apart from everybody else.

Here are four of them.

Jesus Is God

There are only 1,600 people in the world who can claim the title of *billionaire*. Yep, there are only 1,600 billionaires out of 7.1 *billion* humans. There are even fewer who can say they've been president of the United States—forty-three as of this writing (remember that Grover Cleveland was elected twice, but nonconsecutively). And a mere twelve humans can say they've walked on the moon. That's right; just a *dozen* have had their footprints immortalized in moon dust.

But only *one* man is God. . .and that man is Jesus.

Granted, there have been plenty of folks down through history who have *claimed* to be God, but only one man made such a compelling argument for His case. For example, He performed miracles—sometimes in front of thousands of witnesses— dozens of which were recorded and circulated in the Gospels. Most people have heard about Jesus healing people (Matthew 9:18–34), or walking on water (Matthew 14:22–33), or even raising the dead to life (John 11:1–44). But further evidence of Jesus' divinity was His life (lived out in the New Testament) as a fulfillment of various prophecies written down hundreds of years earlier (in the Old Testament). Take a quick look at two of those prophecies:

> *Therefore the Lord himself will give you a sign:*
> *The virgin will conceive and give birth to a son,*
> *and will call him Immanuel. (Isaiah 7:14)*

In accordance with this prophecy, Jesus' mother, Mary, was still a virgin when Jesus was born (Matthew 1:18–25). Though Jesus was raised by Joseph, His father was God. This means that Jesus wasn't born with intrinsic sin in His life like the rest of us. Furthermore, as Isaiah predicted roughly seven hundred years before Jesus visited Earth, He was called Immanuel at His birth (again, see Matthew 1:18–25). Here's another prophecy about Jesus from Isaiah:

> *He was despised and rejected by mankind, a man*
> *of suffering, and familiar with pain. Like one*
> *from whom people hide their faces he was despised,*
> *and we held him in low esteem. (Isaiah 53:3)*

Jesus despised? God rejected? What's this about suffering and pain? It's true; even though Jesus is God, when He came to Earth, He was rejected by the very ones He created and loved. Look at what a man named John, a close friend of Jesus', said about Him:

*He [Jesus] was in the world, and though the
world was made through him, the world did
not recognize him. He came to that which was
his own, but his own did not receive him. (John
1:10–11)*

But it isn't just fulfilled prophecies that point to Jesus as God. Even some of His many enemies became His followers and claimed He was God. One of those former enemies was a man named Saul, who hated Jesus so much that he imprisoned and persecuted anybody who followed Him. But when Saul met Jesus face-to-face (see Acts 9:1–19), it was an eye-opening— or should I say an *eye-closing*—experience. After Jesus radically changed Saul's life, He changed his name, as well. Saul became Paul and went on to serve Jesus for the rest of his life. Through His unlimited power, Jesus equipped Paul to teach the truth about Him, start churches on multiple continents, and perform miracles. Paul's writings about Jesus became a large part of the New Testament, and within his writings are five of the most profound sentences ever put on paper. Take a look at what Paul said about Jesus in the book of Colossians that shows just how special Jesus really is:

*The Son is the image of the invisible God, the
firstborn over all creation. For in him all things
were created: things in heaven and on earth,
visible and invisible, whether thrones or powers or
rulers or authorities; all things have been created*

> *through him and for him. He is before all things,*
> *and in him all things hold together. And he is the*
> *head of the body, the church; he is the beginning*
> *and the firstborn from among the dead, so that in*
> *everything he might have the supremacy. For God*
> *was pleased to have all his fullness dwell in him,*
> *and through him to reconcile to himself all things,*
> *whether things on earth or things in heaven, by*
> *making peace through his blood, shed on the cross.*
> *(Colossians 1:15–20)*

Look at how Paul described Jesus. He called Jesus the "image of the invisible God." In other words, Jesus *literally* shows us what God looks like. In fact, Paul went even further and said that Jesus didn't just show us what God *looks* like; He revealed God in His entirety! "God was pleased to have all his fullness dwell in him," is how Paul put it. Think about the authority that line commands: *the God of the universe was pleased to be known as Jesus.* God hasn't said that about anyone else who's lived on this planet.

That's because Jesus is the only one who is God.

Let's keep going. Everybody knows that God = Creator. So, if Jesus = God, it must also be true that Jesus = Creator. That's *exactly* what Paul said about Jesus. He supported his revelation of Jesus as God by mentioning His role in creation: "By Him [Jesus] all things were created."

Now ponder this: Jesus, the God who created all things, actually took on the form of His creation. He willfully chose to lower Himself and take on the nature of that which He created! Henry Ford, the revolutionary mind behind the motor company that bears his name, never became a Model T (or even a Mustang). Steve Jobs, the tech genius who made Apple a household name, never became an iPhone. But Jesus became a man to show mankind who God is and what He's like.

The Incarnation

Incarnation is the act whereby "God took on the flesh" of humans. In the Incarnation, God joined us. . .as one of us! But Jesus wasn't half man and half God. (What use would we have for a half-god anyway?) No, through the perfect union of the Incarnation, Jesus was 100 percent Man and 100 percent God. Because He was fully a man, Jesus knew what it was like to grow, cry, laugh, face temptation, and more. But because He was also fully God, He was born without sin and lived perfectly without ever committing sin.

When John, Jesus' friend and disciple, talked about God "taking on flesh," he described it this way:

> *The Word [a nickname or title for Jesus] became*
> *flesh and made his dwelling among us. We have*
> *seen his glory, the glory of the one and only Son,*
> *who came from the Father, full of grace and truth.*
> *(John 1:14)*

God, the Creator of all flesh, actually became flesh. It's difficult to ponder that reality without our jaws dropping to the floor. Of course, God ran a huge risk in becoming like us. Let's face it; there are certain liabilities that come with being human. Humans get hurt. Our bones break. We bleed. We die. Jesus knew all that and yet He *still* became flesh. Why did He do it? Why did almighty God choose to take on flesh with all its weaknesses?

That's simple: *so He could die.*

Jesus Died to Save Sinners

Most people die from disease, old age, home improvement projects gone awry, or from running with the bulls. But not Jesus. He died on a cross, an ancient form of capital punishment. He died to forgive people of their sins against God.

Quite literally, Jesus was born to die.

We'll talk much more about this part of Jesus' life (and death) in chapter 5, but for now, let's take another look at the last of those five sentences that Paul wrote:

> *For God was pleased to have all his fullness dwell in him, and through him to reconcile to himself all things, whether things on earth or things in heaven, by making peace through his blood, shed on the cross. (Colossians 1:19–20)*

Jesus' main objective on Earth was to *reconcile* sinners with God—that is, to restore the relationship between sinful humans and God. Unfortunately, you and I are among those sinners who need to be reconciled to God, because our sins—those willfully disobedient thoughts, words, and actions that we commit against God, others, and ourselves—actually separate us from God. For example, when we lie, steal, give in to greed, or commit sexual immorality, we deeply offend God, and that offense carries a price with it. . .a very steep price. God considers our sin so treasonous that it actually demands—and *deserves*—death. (We'll talk *much* more about this reality, as well, in chapter 5.)

But Paul said that Jesus reconciles us to God by "making peace through his blood." In the Old Testament, a person's sins were forgiven by God when the blood of an animal was sacrificed to Him. The blood of Jesus is very special because it is the blood of the Son of God, which means it is untainted by sin. Though the blood of *a lamb* would be used by God to forgive *a person*, the blood of *the Lamb of God* was used by God to forgive *the entire world*.

Atonement

Atonement is a fancy term that describes the payment Jesus made for our sin. In short, our sin requires our death (our "blood"). But Jesus, the "Lamb of God who takes away the sin of the world" (John 1:29), chose to shed His own blood for us by dying on the cross. He literally died in our place and fully paid the debt we owed to God. Because Jesus gave His life in payment for our sins, we are no longer separated from God. Jesus' death and resurrection restored our peace with God. Through His shed blood, Jesus Christ offers us "at-one-ment" with God.

To understand how important the blood of Jesus is for you and me, we need to take a look at a theologically profound movie, *Pirates of the Caribbean: The Curse of the Black Pearl*.

Trust me.

When we meet the evil Captain Barbossa and his band of

miscreants, they have a problem. *A big problem.* They are under the curse of heathen gods because they stole sacred gold. The only way for the curse to be lifted was for every piece of gold to be returned to its original chest. . .*and for each guilty pirate to make a sacrifice of his blood.*

After years of searching for the gold, Barbossa and his crew are close to having the curse lifted. They need just one last gold coin. . .and the blood of William "Bootstraps" Turner, one of the guilty pirates. Unfortunately for the cursed pirates, Old Bootstraps was dead, so a search was under way for his child, because that child would have Bootstraps's blood flowing in his or her veins. Thinking that Elizabeth Swann was Bootstraps's daughter, the pirates kidnap her and take the gold coin from her. But when they draw her blood by cutting her hand over the chest of gold, the curse doesn't lift.

That's because Elizabeth's blood isn't the blood they need.

As everybody who's seen the movie knows, the blood they *really* need is that of Will Turner, the true child of "Bootstraps" Bill Turner. Only after Will sheds his blood does the curse lift.

Likewise, only the blood of Jesus can lift the curse of sin on us.

Jesus shed His blood "on the cross," a ghastly and torturous device created to make its victims suffer as much as possible before ultimately dying a cruel and humiliating death. The carnage inflicted on the human body was terrifyingly graphic. Oftentimes, as in Jesus' case, crucifixion followed a vicious beating. Then long spikes were driven through the victim's hands and feet. Slowly and painfully, the victim would begin

Christianity. . .It's Like This

to lose vital body fluids, experience dehydration, and suffocate. The condemned often gasped for air because, unless they were able to push upward with their legs (which in any case they would eventually become exhausted), their body weight rested completely on the arms and shoulders until they were pulled from their sockets, eventually forcing all the victim's weight onto the chest muscles. Breathing became difficult and shallow until it eventually ceased altogether.

This is the kind of death Jesus suffered. But His death was far from pointless. In fact, His death was the most significant in history, because He chose to die for sinners.

Fortunately, that's not where Jesus' story ends.

Jesus Came Back to Life

After Jesus died the horrifying death described above, He was hastily buried in a tomb that belonged to a friend of His. It didn't matter that the tomb was a borrowed one; Jesus wasn't going to need it for very long, anyway.

Three days after He died and was buried, Jesus was resurrected—*He rose from the dead.*

As you might guess, a lot rides on this part of Jesus' life. To say that the resurrection of Jesus is crucial to the Christian faith is a major understatement. In fact, Paul placed the Resurrection at the very center of our faith:

> *If Christ has not been raised, your faith is futile;*
> *you are still in your sins. Then those also who have*

75

> *fallen asleep in Christ are lost. If only for this life*
> *we have hope in Christ, we are of all people most*
> *to be pitied. (1 Corinthians 15:17–19)*

Paul said that if the resurrection of Jesus *isn't* true, if Jesus really *didn't* rise from the dead, then Christians are the most misguided and disappointed people in the world. No argument there. Christians have a lot riding on the resurrection of Jesus.

For starters, if Jesus didn't rise from the dead, it would make Him a liar, because He actually predicted that He would be killed *and* raised three days later. In fact, He talked about His resurrection a lot (see Mark 8:31; 9:31; and 10:33–34 for a few examples). If Jesus didn't rise from the dead, it would mean that the grave is the end and there is no life after death. If Jesus didn't rise from the dead, we would have no hope.

But Jesus did rise from the dead. Paul affirmed this truth in his very next line:

> *But Christ has indeed been raised from the dead,*
> *the firstfruits of those who have fallen asleep. For*
> *since death came through a man, the resurrection*
> *of the dead comes also through a man. For as in*
> *Adam all die, so in Christ all will be made alive.*
> *(1 Corinthians 15:20–22)*

I freely confess that the resurrection of Jesus is the part of Christianity that requires the most faith. Christians believe that a dead man came back to life. That's not natural.

But neither is God. He's supernatural.

No one can prove that the Resurrection happened; but neither can anyone prove that it *didn't* happen. There are lots of reasons for believing that the Resurrection is a historical fact: there were eyewitnesses; the opposition's version of the story has lots and lots of holes in it; and the disciples' lives were completely changed by the fact that Jesus overcame the grave. Almost all of those men who walked with Jesus and believed in His resurrection lost their lives for talking about it. If they'd known that the Resurrection was a hoax, surely those men would have lost their nerve when confronted with death; no one is willing to die for a lie. Blaise Pascal famously said, "I believe those witnesses who get their throats cut."

Me too.

I have no trouble believing that Jesus came back to life, because He brought *others* back to life (see Luke 7:11–16 and John 11:38–45 for just a *couple* of examples). However, the question of whether or not Jesus came back to life isn't *nearly* as puzzling to me as why He died for me (and you) in the first place.

The bottom line is simple: If the Resurrection isn't true, then Jesus was the biggest joke ever to walk the earth. If the Resurrection isn't true, then Jesus was a fool, and so is every single one of His followers.

But make no mistake, if the Resurrection *is* true, then everything Jesus said must be taken seriously.

Including what He said will happen in the future.

Jesus Will Return to Judge the Entire World

It's very difficult to describe events that haven't taken place yet. For instance, nobody knows who will win next year's Super Bowl or World Series, mainly because we don't even know which teams will be playing in those championship games. We also don't know who our next president will be, as important as that is. There's so much about the future we just don't know.

But there's one future event you can—and should—bet your life on: *the return of Jesus Christ.*

We've already talked about Jesus' *first* coming, the Incarnation, when God "took on flesh" and became a man so He could die for the sins of the world. But during that time, Jesus frequently spoke about His *second* coming, or His *return*, in which He will establish His eternal kingdom and judge everyone who has ever been born. Granted, that was roughly two thousand years ago, and He hasn't appeared yet, but if Jesus is who He said He is—and that looks to be the case—then His return is an absolute certainty.

Not only did Jesus talk about His second coming, but *every* writer in the New Testament did as well. One of Jesus' main teachings about His return can be found in Matthew 24 and 25. The text is too long to insert here, but I strongly encourage you to take about six minutes to read those two chapters in Matthew's Gospel; you'll see that Jesus described His return in graphic, and sometimes unsettling, terms. In addition to the cataclysmic descriptions of His second coming, Jesus also offered a few stories that drive home several unmistakable points.

First, we learn that Jesus is going to personally return in the same way He went to heaven the first time (Acts 1:9–11). He isn't going to send an angelic ambassador, nor will His presence be reduced to some sort of heavenly vision. No, He's coming back in the same flesh He put on at His first coming. Jesus even says that we will see Him and hear Him (Matthew 24:30–31). In fact, Jesus' presence will be so undeniable that "all the peoples of the earth" will note His return (Matthew 24:30).

Second, we learn that Jesus will return with "power and great glory" (Matthew 24:30). He will be accompanied by angels and His authority will be unlimited and unimaginable. When Jesus came the first time, He was a humble Lamb who was willing to give His life for others. When He returns, He will be a fierce Lion (Revelation 5:5) who is not just the matchless King of the jungle, but the unparalleled King of the universe. Of course, there's a reason why Jesus is coming back with such power and authority.

It's because, third, we learn that Jesus is coming back to judge all mankind. Don't misunderstand this; Jesus isn't just going to judge Christians or good people or religious people. He's going to judge every single person who has ever lived. Let me translate "every single person who has ever lived": it means *everybody*. Buddhists. Muslims. Atheists. African tribesmen. Kings and kindergarten teachers, good guys and gangsters, murderers and millionaires. Every person in human history will stand before Jesus and be judged. Jesus is going to do a *lot* of judging!

Maybe that wrecks your notion of Jesus. Maybe you think Jesus is just a really nice guy who simply lets everybody do their own thing. Most people like the idea of Nice Jesus. Hardly anybody likes the idea of Judge Jesus...*including a lot of Christians*. But let me explain why you really need (and want) Judge Jesus.

Think about all the Jews that Hitler killed during the Holocaust. Think about all the spouses who've been victims of domestic abuse. Think about all the kids who've been enslaved in sweatshops around the world. Think about all the searching people who were cheated out of their money (and souls) by some charlatan posing as a preacher. Think about every person who was wounded by gossip. The list could go on and on and on. Wouldn't a just God be concerned with righting those wrongs?

On the opposite side of the same coin, think about the love and sacrifice of godly parents on behalf of their children. Think about the faithfulness of missionaries who served God in desolate and dangerous regions far from their homes. Think about the recovering drug addict or alcoholic who has placed complete trust in Christ for freedom. Again, the list could go on for a long time. Shouldn't a loving God be concerned with rewarding their perseverance?

Of course He should! And because Jesus is Judge, that's exactly what He will do. He will reward the righteous, those who've invested their lives in following Him, and He will punish the unrighteous, those who've rejected His teaching,

His love, and His forgiveness.

Finally, we learn that Jesus is coming back to establish His eternal kingdom. Every King has a kingdom; Jesus is no different. Part of Jesus' agenda at His second coming will be to usher in the kingdom of God that He spent so much time talking about during His time on earth. This kingdom will be unlike every other kingdom the world has ever seen. Its King will not be a flawed man, but a perfect and flawless God; its citizens will not be plagued with sickness, disease, violence, or corruption. Its length will be without end, and the Prince of Peace, another of Jesus' titles, will reign over all. (We'll talk more about this in chapter 7.)

None Like Jesus

No other person in the world possesses any of Jesus' supernatural attributes, let alone all four of them. But Jesus can make a claim to these and more! That's why there has never been, and never will be, another person like Jesus. He's just too special.

It only takes a glance across our culture to see that Jesus gets a bad rap these days. Some call Him "intolerant" or "exclusive" for saying He is the only way to heaven (see John 14:6). He's neither. Some label Jesus as "confused" or "contradictory" because of the nature of His teaching. Again, He's neither. Some have even labeled Jesus as "powerless" because of the number of blind, lame, and sick people who go uncured these days when He healed so many blind, lame, and sick people long ago. It's hard to make that label fit a man who gave His life on a cross, took it back up again, and changed the entire world.

The list of accusations is a long one. I simply encourage you to examine Jesus closely for yourself. Anyone who is willing to die for you deserves, at the very least, a simple investigation into who and what He claims to be.

If you sincerely look for Jesus, He *will* reveal Himself to you. You'll find that not only is He God, but He's so wildly in love with you that He'd rather die *for* you than live *without* you.

Jesus. There's just nobody else like Him.

Session 3

Jesus

What makes Him so special?

Big Idea: Jesus gave His life to save people from their sin.
Passage: Romans 5:6–11
Discussion Starter: *Abraham Lincoln: He Died for Me*

Nobody noticed the crazed gunman sneak into Ford's Theater the night Lincoln was shot, but many thousands saw the president's body as it journeyed by train from Washington, D.C. to Springfield, Illinois, where it was laid to final rest. The home stretch of Lincoln's earthly travels deeply affected the grateful people of a grieving nation.

Especially one anonymous woman from New York.

In the hours following the news of the president's assassination, the highest ranking government leaders decided that Lincoln's body should "tour" several states in the Union that he had just saved from civil war. Mayors of every city and governors from every state requested a stop in their respective districts; of course, the train couldn't stop at every junction across America, but wherever it did, thousands of slaves, politicians, widows, woodcutters (Lincoln's first occupation), and other common folk poured into the streets to catch a glimpse of the man who had saved America.

When Lincoln's body arrived in New York City in late April 1865, several interesting—*almost conflicting*—remarks were overheard by mourners in the crowd. They were recorded by historians and biographers and passed down to us:

> *As [Lincoln's body] reached Canal Street a woman leaning from a tenement window called out, "Well, is that all that's left of Ould Abe?" Her strident voice carried afar in the solemn hush. A bystander looked up and retorted, "It's more than you'll ever be!" "O, I've nothing against him," she responded without rancor. "I never knew him or cared for him, but he died like a saint," she exclaimed and crossed herself in respect. A white-haired [African American woman] held an apron to her face and between sobs wailed, "He died for me! He was crucified for me! God bless him!"* [1]

How that crowd saw Lincoln then is almost identical to how people see Jesus today. Some look at the Son of God and say, "I didn't really know Him, and to be honest, I don't have much need of Him."

Others see the same man and exclaim, "He died for me!"

Opening Questions

1. Everybody knows at least *something* about Abraham Lincoln. What made him so special?

2. The reports from above reveal that there were differences of opinion about President Lincoln. Why do you think that was?

3. There are lots of conflicting opinions about Jesus. What are some of the ones you've heard about Him? Why do you think those conflicts exist?

4. What did the African American woman mean when she said of Abraham Lincoln, "He died for me"?

5. Without a doubt, Abraham Lincoln was a special man. In your opinion, is there anything that makes Jesus special? If so, what?

Bible Passage

Romans 5:6–11

> *You see, at just the right time, when we were still powerless, Christ died for the ungodly. Very rarely will anyone die for a righteous person, though for a good person someone might possibly dare to die. But God demonstrates his own love for us in this: While we were still sinners, Christ died for us.*

*Since we have now been justified by his blood,
how much more shall we be saved from God's
wrath through him! For if, while we were God's
enemies, we were reconciled to him through the
death of his Son, how much more, having been
reconciled, shall we be saved through his life! Not
only is this so, but we also boast in God through
our Lord Jesus Christ, through whom we have
now received reconciliation.*

Study Questions

1. Very specifically, how did God demonstrate His love for us?

2. According to this passage, Jesus does a lot on behalf of sinners. What are some of the things Jesus did for us?

3. What did it cost Jesus for us to be "justified" by God and "reconciled to Him"? (Hint: Check out verses 9 and 10.)

Deeper Questions

1. In this passage, we are called "powerless," "ungodly," "sinners," and "God's enemies." Why are we described in such negative terms?

2. What is sin, and why does God take sin so seriously that Jesus had to die to save us from it?

3. Why is it important for us to be "justified" before God and "reconciled" to Him? What happens to us if we aren't?

4. In chapter 1, we learned that God not only exists, but He loves us, as well. How does this passage from Romans reinforce the fact that God loves us?

Application Questions

1. In Romans 3:23, we're told that we're all sinners. This means we've all alienated ourselves from God and deserve death for how we've lived. If that's truly the case—and the Bible only tells the truth—then what sin(s) does Jesus need to save you from?

2. Have you asked Jesus to save you from your sin(s)? If so, when? If not, why not?

3. How did your life change after you asked Jesus to save you from your sin. . .or how would your life change if you were to ask Jesus to save you from your sin?

Final Word

It's impossible to overstate the importance of Jesus Christ to Christianity. After all, the faith gets its name from Him! But don't miss the importance of Jesus Christ to *you*. Jesus is the only one who can save us from our sins, thereby pardoning us of our guilt before God.

If you want to know how important a pardon is, just ask James Porter and George Wilson.

In December 1829, Porter and Wilson robbed several postal shipments and terrorized various mail carriers in their rampage for loot. Unfortunately for them, they were soon caught, tried, and condemned to hang for their crimes. Porter was hanged on schedule; Wilson was given a pardon.

But in the end, ironically, Wilson, too, was hanged for his crimes.

In the span of five short months, the two men had robbed the United States mail, been tried and found guilty of their crimes, and were facing justice at the end of a rope. On July 2, 1830, James Porter walked up the gallows, and shortly thereafter, into eternity.

George Wilson didn't share Porter's fate, even though he shared his guilt. That's because Wilson had several influential friends, and they petitioned President Andrew Jackson on his behalf. The president, who was known as Old Hickory, listened to their case and granted a presidential pardon to the guilty man. Instead of facing the gallows, Wilson was sentenced to twenty years in prison.

But then something very strange happened: *Wilson declined President Jackson's pardon.*

This had never happened before. Here was a man who'd been condemned to die for his crimes against the government, rescued by none other than the president of the United States, and yet he wouldn't accept the gracious pardon. Stunned, those involved in the case asked Wilson to explain himself, but the prisoner had nothing else to say.

The government was now in a quandary as to what to do with George Wilson. The case was in the headlines of many papers and attracted the attention of every lawyer in the nation. US Attorney General Roger Taney weighed in on the case and said, "The court cannot give the prisoner the benefit of the pardon unless he claims the benefit of it. It is a grant to him; and he may accept it or not, as he pleases."

Chief Justice John Marshall had the responsibility of delivering the final verdict. In his lengthy statement to the court—and the rest of the nation—he wisely noted, "A pardon is a deed, to the validity of which delivery is essential, and delivery is not complete without acceptance. It may then be rejected by the person to whom it is tendered; and if it be rejected, we have discovered no power in a court to force it on him."[2]

Because George Wilson had rejected the pardon he remained under the penalty of death and was soon hanged for his crimes.

Wilson was foolish to commit the crime, and even more foolish to decline the pardon from President Jackson. But there are a lot of people who are even more foolish than George Wilson because they reject the pardon that God offers them from their sins.

Have you accepted the pardon that God wants to extend to you through His Son, Jesus Christ?

4

The Holy Spirit

Why does everyone think He's so weird?

Our culture has an affinity for *weird*.

We're so enamored with weirdness that we create it... and then celebrate it. For instance, what other society could conceive of the likes of Lady Gaga? The "Mother Monster," who's sold more than a hundred million singles worldwide not only admits to smoking marijuana while writing her music, but then wears a dress made of raw meat to accept awards for it. Lady Gaga even splits her stage time with a male alter ego she devised named Jo Calderone.

You gotta admit, that's a little weird.

Then there's Robert John Burck, aka the Naked Cowboy. I've bumped into him. . .*literally*. Let's just say that when you run into a large man in Times Square, at night, who is wearing nothing but a pair of boots, a cowboy hat, and some tighty whities, your life is changed.

And dare I bring up Dennis Rodman, the man with so

many body piercings he's become a human pin cushion? To attract attention for the release of his book *Bad As I Wanna Be*, the former NBA champ donned a white wedding dress. You have my word: I will *not* resort to the same strategy to market this book. You're welcome.

Let's be honest. These iconic figures are a bit *weird*. Something about their image, their reputation, or their actions cause us to ponder their credibility. But these cultural icons aren't the only ones with the distinction of being labeled weird; the Holy Spirit is often dubbed that, as well. Perhaps you've heard the banter:

- *"Kinda spooky if you ask me. After all, His name is the Holy Ghost, right?"*

- *"I've seen that Holy Spirit stuff on TV—slaying in the Spirit. Definitely not for me."*

- *"The Holy Spirit? Isn't that when Christians start talking all mumbo jumbo?"*

For many reasons, the Holy Spirit is clouded in misunderstanding—one of which is the way we refer to Him. The identities of God the *Father* and God the *Son* seem more easily understood (if only because our earthly families include fathers and sons). But the Holy Spirit? What's that? It's little wonder many treat Him like a mysterious stranger.

Consequently, the Holy Spirit is often the most confusing (and hotly debated) point of doctrine in all of Christianity.

But that doesn't have to be the case; Scripture is perfectly clear about the Holy Spirit, and if we search it, we'll discover that the Holy Spirit isn't weird at all.

Introducing. . .the Holy Spirit

Here's how the Bible reveals the Holy Spirit: *He is God who lives in us to glorify Jesus.* Okay, I know that's a lot, so let's break it down bit by bit, starting with the fact that the Holy Spirit is God.

If you grab a Bible and flip through its pages looking for the phrase *Holy Spirit,* you'll find the letter *s* capitalized every time. There's a reason for that: the writers of the Bible considered the Holy Spirit a person—just like William or Jessica or Napoleon Dynamite—and capitalized the proper noun every time. (Their sixth-grade grammar teachers would be so proud.) Of course, that simply means the Holy Spirit is a person, but not necessarily God; after all, there are plenty of real people who aren't God. But if we look at *what* this person has done, we'll get a better idea of *who* He is.

For starters, the Holy Spirit was active in Creation. Listen to what the first two verses of the Bible say about the beginning—you know, that part of the universe's timeline when nothing and no one existed except God:

> *In the beginning God created the heavens and the earth. Now the earth was formless and empty, darkness was over the surface of the deep, and the Spirit of God was hovering over the waters.*
> *(Genesis 1:1–2)*

Did you catch that? The Spirit of God—one of the Holy Spirit's many names—was there, in the beginning, with God! *Umm. . .how could He be there at that time if He's not God?*

The Trinity

The Trinity—God the Father, God the Son, and God the Holy Spirit—is difficult to understand. In fact, St. Augustine once famously said, "If you deny the Trinity, you will lose your soul. If you try to understand the Trinity, you will lose your mind." Even though the word Trinity is never found in Scripture, the Bible points several times to the existence of the Trinity, most clearly at Jesus' baptism (Matthew 3:13-17), and again in the Great Commission (Matthew 28:19-20). And no, there aren't any accurate illustrations to describe the Trinity, including the three-leaf clover one, the H2O one, the egg one, or any other one; they all have flaws. Sorry, the Trinity is completely unlike anything else in the universe (because God is, too). God is revealed in three persons—Father, Son, and Spirit—but not three different Gods. God is three-in-one. Each person in the Trinity is distinct from the others, yet the exact same in essence, and completely equal in power, glory, and majesty. Yep, Augustine was right.

Unfortunately, many Christians *wrongly* believe that the Holy Spirit came into existence on the Day of Pentecost, which is mentioned in the New Testament book of Acts. That's not the case at all. The Holy Spirit is God because He has *always* existed! In spite of what we discussed in the last chapter, many of the same believers make a similar mistake regarding Jesus; they think Jesus didn't exist until He was born in a manger, an event that is also chronicled in the New Testament. But Jesus and the Holy Spirit have always existed—since *before* the beginning—and that means they are both just as much *God* as is the Father.

Scripture clearly tells us that the Holy Spirit was active in creation, and since creating is an act of God, as we've already seen in chapter 1, we have a strong reason to conclude that the Holy Spirit is God. But there are plenty more reasons to believe that the Holy Spirit is God.

For example, the Holy Spirit played a crucial role in giving us God's words. In 2 Peter 1:20–21 the apostle writes:

> *Above all, you must understand that no prophecy of Scripture came about by the prophet's own interpretation. For prophecy never had its origin in the human will, but prophets, though human, spoke from God as they were carried along by the Holy Spirit.*

Peter tells us that Scripture doesn't have its origin in humanity, but in God. That's simple enough. The ancient message given by the prophets in the Old Testament and the teaching given by the disciples/apostles in the New Testament did not come from them, but from God Himself. Further, Peter tells us that these people were under the influence of the Holy Spirit. Since only God can give us His words, we have another reason to conclude that the Holy Spirit is God.

But let's look at one more supernatural work the Holy Spirit has accomplished. If any doubt remains that the Holy Spirit is God, this should clear it up. We see in Scripture that the Holy Spirit played an instrumental role in Jesus' resurrection. In fact, Romans 8:11 clearly states that the Holy Spirit is the one who raised Jesus from the dead:

> *If the Spirit of him [God] who raised Jesus from the dead is living in you, he who raised Christ from the dead will also give life to your mortal bodies because of his Spirit who lives in you.*

In this passage, the apostle Paul says that it was the Holy Spirit—God—who raised Jesus from the dead. As we learned in chapter 3, the act of resurrection is something so exclusive that only God can accomplish it. No doctor, no matter how specialized in medicine he or she may be, can bring a dead person back to life. A miracle (like resurrection) requires a miracle worker: *God.* And in this passage, Paul says that the miracle-working God is none other than the Holy Spirit.

By the way, in his world-changing sermon on the Day of Pentecost, the apostle Peter, who had just been filled with the Holy Spirit, stood up in front of thousands in downtown Jerusalem and talked about the resurrection of Jesus:

> *God has raised this Jesus to life, and we are all witnesses of it. (Acts 2:32)*

Paul said that Jesus was raised from the dead by the Holy Spirit. Peter said Jesus was raised by God. They aren't contradicting one another; they are simply referring to the same person, the Holy Spirit, who is God.

Given that the Holy Spirit is God, could we do Him (and

ourselves) a favor and stop calling Him "it"? You wouldn't refer to any other person as an "it." If you say of a woman, "*It's* wearing a black dress," you'll probably be wearing a black eye! The Holy Spirit is not an *it*. He's a *He*! We need to speak to Him as a *person*, for that is exactly what He is: *a person who also happens to be God*.

So far, nothing stands out as totally weird about the Holy Spirit. But where He chooses to live has raised more than a few eyebrows....

A Unique Dwelling Place

Earth's surface is dotted with temples, structures that were built hundreds—if not thousands—of years ago to honor various gods. The marble columns of the mighty Parthenon, built to honor the goddess Athena, are striking for sure, but the majesty of that 2,500-year-old building pales in comparison to newer, more ornate temples. For example, the Buddhist temple known as the Shwedagon Pagoda in Myanmar is covered in gold, and its spire, which points heavenward, is adorned with more than five thousand diamonds and two thousand rubies. Another Buddhist temple, Wat Rong Khun, more commonly known as the White Temple, in Thailand, gleams in the sunlight thanks to its construction of whitewashed stone and mirror flakes. Cambodia's world-renowned Angkor Wat, which means City of Temples, is the world's largest temple, encompassing more than two hundred acres of walls, pools, courtyards, and towers.

Though these temples stem from different religious beliefs,

they have one thing in common: *people go to them to connect with their gods.*

The Holy Spirit distinguishes Himself from all these gods—who are not gods at all, by the way—by dwelling in a place that is far less ornate and majestic. Instead of living in palaces with marble halls or towering temples with grandiose landscapes, the Holy Spirit has chosen to live within *us.* At least, that's what Jesus teaches in John 14:15–17:

> *"If you love me, keep my commands. And I will ask the Father, and he will give you another advocate to help you and be with you forever— the Spirit of truth. The world cannot accept him, because it neither sees him nor knows him. But you know him, for he lives with you and will be in you."*

In this passage—which is another that refers to the Trinity without actually using the word—Jesus says that anyone who loves Him will know the Holy Spirit (called the "Spirit of truth" in this passage), because the Father will give us the Holy Spirit to live *in* us. Think about that for a moment: the mighty God who created the world has decided to live in fragile humans, not massive structures of wood and stone decorated in costly and precious jewels. *God the Spirit lives in us!*

In 1 Corinthians 6:19, the apostle Paul says that our bodies are "temples of the Holy Spirit." It can be daunting to try to wrap our measly three-pound brains around the concept of

God living within us, but it's true. Maybe the reason why the Holy Spirit chose to dwell in us has something to do with God's desire for us to live holy lives and His constant pursuit of us.

You see, in the Old Testament, God the Father is portrayed as living *above* us. We're told in Exodus 31:18 that God met with Moses at the top of Mount Sinai to give him the law so that God's people would know how to live their lives in a way that pleased Him. Unfortunately, Moses and all the rest of us broke God's law. . .*so God took a step closer to us.*

Then God came down from heaven and revealed Himself as Jesus, God *beside* us. In Matthew 1:23, we're told that Jesus' alternate name, Immanuel, actually means "God with us." Jesus walked with us, taught us, and performed miracles among us. Tragically, we chose to crucify Jesus. . .*so God took yet another step closer.*

Finally, God sent His Spirit to live *within* those who are committed to following Jesus. The writer of Hebrews puts it this way:

> *The Holy Spirit also testifies to us about this. First he says: "This is the covenant I will make with them after that time, says the Lord. I will put my laws in their hearts, and I will write them on their minds." (Hebrews 10:15–16)*

Through the Holy Spirit, God has changed who we are on the inside, in our very hearts and minds. The Holy Spirit is God *in* us. God cannot get any closer *to* us than *in* us!

This doesn't mean that we become gods ourselves, just because the Holy Spirit lives in us. When a virus or a bacterium lives in us, we don't become a virus or a bacterium; we become sick! But when the Holy Spirit lives in us, we are supernaturally empowered to do something that has eternal significance.

The Holy Spirit: Hype Man Extraordinaire?

I'm not a fan of mainline hip-hop, because it's usually filled with obscene and vulgar language, demeaning attitudes toward women, and enough references to drugs and alcohol to give Snoop Dogg a buzz. That said, today's hip-hop icons make use of something called a "hype man" that can help us understand the Holy Spirit's purpose in our lives.

A hype man is a member of the rapper's posse who's tasked with making sure the crowd is focused on the rapper. Sometimes the hype man is a lesser-known backup singer, and sometimes the hype man is another full-fledged rapper; regardless, his job is the same: *make the star shine as bright as possible.*

That's what the Holy Spirit does for Jesus; He *glorifies* Jesus. Remember what we've been saying about the Holy Spirit all along: *the Holy Spirit is God who lives in us to glorify Jesus.* In John 16:12–14, Jesus describes the Holy Spirit's work in the following way:

> *I have much more to say to you, more than you can now bear. But when he, the Spirit of truth, comes, he will guide you into all the truth. He will*

> *not speak on his own; he will speak only what he*
> *hears, and he will tell you what is yet to come. He*
> *will glorify me because it is from me that he will*
> *receive what he will make known to you.*

Like a good hype man, the Holy Spirit puts the focus on Jesus and makes sure He is the center of everyone's attention, including ours. In this passage, Jesus says that the Holy Spirit, again called the Spirit of Truth, will guide His disciples into all truth *and* bring glory to Jesus *by taking what "is from [Jesus]" and making it "known to you"* (John 16:14). Everything the Holy Spirit does in our lives is for the purpose of glorifying Jesus.

And the Holy Spirit does a lot in the lives of believers to glorify Jesus.

For starters, the Holy Spirit guides us into *all* the truth so we can know Jesus and follow Him. Because we cannot follow someone we don't understand, the Holy Spirit helps us understand the truth about Jesus so we can live our lives in a way that honors Him. When followers of Jesus think, speak, and act the way He commanded us to, He is glorified by our lives. But that would be impossible for us to do without the Holy Spirit *guiding* us in truth. It's just one way the Holy Spirit glorifies Jesus in us.

Another way the Holy Spirit glorifies Jesus in our lives is by giving us spiritual gifts to serve Him and others. First Corinthians 12:11 says these gifts (such as wisdom, faith, and prophecy) are given directly by the Holy Spirit: "*All these [gifts]*

David R. Smith

are the work of one and the same Spirit, and he distributes them to each one, just as he determines."

When we use our spiritual gifts to serve God and help others, Jesus is glorified. But we wouldn't have those spiritual gifts if the Holy Spirit didn't give them to us.

But the Holy Spirit does more than just guide us in truth and give us gifts; He is also our source of supernatural power. All across the pages of Scripture, we see God's Holy Spirit empowering those who put their trust in Him. Samson, the Arnold Schwarzenegger of the Old Testament, got his supernatural strength from the Holy Spirit (Judges 14:6). The Holy Spirit also gave Israel's judges, such as Othniel (Judges 3:10), Gideon (Judges 6:34), and Jephthah (Judges 11:29) victory over their enemies.

The Holy Spirit's miraculous intervention in human affairs also isn't limited to the Old Testament. For example, in the New Testament, He gave the disciples power to do their assigned work (as foretold in Acts 1:8) and helped them spread the good news about Jesus to people of other nations (Acts 2:4–11). The Holy Spirit also helped the disciples overcome the schemes of evil people (Acts 13:9–12) and even predict future events (Acts 11:28). The Holy Spirit enabled God's people to change their world and thereby bring glory to Jesus!

And He wants to do the same through you and me.

Unfortunately, there are obstacles to God's desires; for example, some people want the Holy Spirit to glorify *them*. When the Holy Spirit guides people in truth, instead of humbly applying it to their lives, some try to wield it against others in condescending and judgmental ways. When the Holy Spirit gives spiritual gifts to people, instead of using them to serve the interests of Jesus, some use their gifts to serve their own interests. Likewise, when the Holy Spirit fills people with power, instead of using it to make the name of Jesus great, some use that power to try to make their own name great.

The Holy Spirit won't tolerate this. If He doesn't glorify Himself, He's certainly not going to allow us to glorify ourselves. He is single-minded in His purpose. He is God who lives in us to glorify Jesus, and Jesus alone.

A Bird? A Blaze? A Big Breeze?

Now that we know who the Holy Spirit is (God), where He lives (in us), and what He does (glorifies Jesus), a natural question to ask about the Holy Spirit is this: *What is He like?* A good portion of chapter 1 was invested in finding out what God is like. Almost all of chapter 3 did the same with Jesus. Because the Holy Spirit is also God, let's allow Scripture to describe Him, as well.

Unlike the Father and the Son, the Holy Spirit is personified in Scripture in several ways that are quite different from one another. For example, at Jesus' baptism in the Jordan River, the Holy Spirit is symbolized as a dove that descends and alights on Jesus (Matthew 3:13–17). But on one occasion in Jesus' ministry, when He taught about the Holy Spirit, He used the imagery of water:

On the last and greatest day of the festival, Jesus

> stood and said in a loud voice, "Let anyone who is
> thirsty come to me and drink. Whoever believes in
> me, as Scripture has said, rivers of living water
> will flow from within them." By this he meant
> the Spirit, whom those who believed in him were
> later to receive. (John 7:37–39)

"Living water" is just one symbol Jesus used to describe the
Holy Spirit. After Jesus' return to heaven at the end of His
earthly ministry, the Holy Spirit took a radically different
form on the Day of Pentecost. Look at how the book of Acts
describes His appearance:

> When the day of Pentecost came, they were all
> together in one place. Suddenly a sound like the
> blowing of a violent wind came from heaven and
> filled the whole house where they were sitting.
> They saw what seemed to be tongues of fire that
> separated and came to rest on each of them. All of
> them were filled with the Holy Spirit and began
> to speak in other tongues as the Spirit enabled
> them. (Acts 2:1–4)

In this passage, we see the Holy Spirit described in images of
fire *and* a violent wind. Neither of those have much in common
with peaceful doves. . .or rivers of living water, for that matter.
There are even more symbols used to describe the Holy Spirit
in Scripture, but the number of symbols personifying the Holy

Spirit is short in comparison to the myriad of titles the Bible uses to refer to the Holy Spirit. If you take a few moments to look up the passages in this (abbreviated) list below, you'll have an even better understanding of the Holy Spirit's identity.

- Spirit of God (Genesis 1:2)
- Holy Spirit (Psalm 51:11)
- Spirit of your Father (Matthew 10:19-20)
- Advocate (John 14:16)
- Spirit of truth (John 14:17)
- Spirit of the Lord (Acts 5:9)
- Spirit of Jesus (Acts 16:7)
- Spirit of holiness (Romans 1:4)
- Spirit of life (Romans 8:2)
- Spirit of adoption (Romans 8:15)
- Spirit of our God (1 Corinthians 6:11)
- Spirit of the living God (2 Corinthians 3:3)
- Spirit of His Son (Galatians 4:6)
- Spirit of wisdom and revelation (Ephesians 1:17)
- Eternal Spirit (Hebrews 9:14)
- Spirit of grace (Hebrews 10:29)
- Spirit of Christ (1 Peter 1:11)
- Spirit of glory (1 Peter 4:14)

Again, this is not a complete list of titles, references, or names of the Holy Spirit. For example, in Isaiah 11:2, the Holy Spirit is referred to as the "*Spirit of the LORD. . .the Spirit of wisdom and of understanding. . .the Spirit of counsel and of might. . .*

the Spirit of knowledge and fear of the LORD.*"* That's four different revelations in one verse!

If we were to synthesize all that the Bible says about the Holy Spirit, we'd discover that one of the best descriptions of the Holy Spirit is "busy." Think about it; the Holy Spirit is living inside every believer, leading, equipping, empowering, teaching, transforming—and much more—so that Jesus will be glorified in us.

And to think, some people regard Him as weird. . . .

Back to the Question

So, why do so many people seem to think the Holy Spirit is weird? It's a complex question, but the answer is quite simple.

Because they don't know Him.

They don't know all He does on behalf of believers. They've never been filled with His presence or equipped by His gifts. They've never known the truth He teaches, because they've been sidelined by one lie after another. Nor have they experienced His world-changing power in their lives. To those who don't know Him, the Holy Spirit remains an impersonal concept that is completely irrelevant to life.

But for those who *do* know the Holy Spirit, He is anything but weird. He is God Himself, who loves us so much He chooses to live within us despite how frail and faithless and sinful we can be. He is the one who generously gives gifts that bless our lives and the lives of others. And He personally shapes us into the image of Jesus by growing our *"love, joy, peace, forbearance, kindness, goodness, faithfulness, gentleness, and self-control"* (Galatians 5:22–23).

In short, the Holy Spirit helps us do the most important thing in life: *live like Jesus.* We cannot do that without the Holy Spirit.

Those who know Him know He's not weird. They know He's God.

Session 4

The Holy Spirit

Why does everyone think He's so weird?

Big Idea: The Holy Spirit empowers believers to serve God and bring glory to Jesus. . .which is what He wants to do through you.

Passage: Acts 4:1–21

Discussion Starter: *The Work of World Changers*

William Carey

Born in England in 1761, William Carey taught himself Latin by age twelve. While apprenticing for a shoemaker, he also learned Greek and French because he knew it wouldn't be long before he switched from fixing soles to saving souls.

Carey was well educated and served his community as a teacher and pastor, but his heart was captivated by foreign missionaries and their crucial work. He challenged his fellow pastors to help with the cause, but they only scolded him: "Sit down, young man, sit down. You are a miserable enthusiast.

Certainly nothing can be done until another Pentecost. . . . When the Lord wants to convert the heathen, He will do it without your help or mine."

Instead, Carey organized a missionary team, and soon thereafter set sail for India with his family to preach the Gospel to the millions who put their trust in gods made of clay, wood, and stone. In that poverty-stricken and superstitious land, William Carey began to work and preach. And work and preach. And work and preach. Seven long years later, he won his first Hindu to Christ.

Today the subcontinent of India still bears the marks of Carey's ministry. India contains one of the largest bodies of Christian believers in the world, and thanks to Carey's diligence in the area of translation, the Bible was made accessible to 300 million people in their native language and dialect.

Martha Myers

Trained as a medical doctor, this courageous woman served God in one of the most volatile regions on earth, the Middle East. Even though she was killed in 2002, the fruit of her life is still affecting Muslims because of a decision she made years earlier.

Even at age nine, Martha knew what she wanted to do with her life. She had become a Christian that year and was soon engrossed in her church's missionary efforts. After high school and college, she attended medical school and eventually settled in Yemen, working long hours at the Jibla Baptist Hospital throughout the week and delivering medical supplies to remote areas on the weekends. Her work was risky; in the late 1990s, she was carjacked by armed men who threatened to kill her.

Such episodes led Martha to make an important decision: She asked her family to allow her to be buried in Yemen if she died there. *Sadly, that's exactly what happened.*

On December 30, 2002, a woman visited the hospital and was treated by Dr. Myers. The grateful woman went home and told her husband about the love and compassion she'd received from the Christian medic. . .something no Muslim doctor had ever given her. Fueled by his radical beliefs and hatred of Christianity, the husband smuggled a rifle into the hospital and killed Dr. Myers, along with two other Baptist missionaries.

But that wasn't the end of Dr. Martha Myers's witness in Yemen.

On the grounds of the hospital where she had served for more than twenty years, there is a marker with her name on it, along with the following inscription: "She loves God." Even in death, she testifies of the power and love of Jesus Christ to those who do not know Him yet.

Adoniram Judson

On February 19, 1812, Adoniram Judson and his wife of seven days, Ann Haseltine, set sail for India with the intentions of evangelizing the subcontinent's mostly Hindu population. But the East India Company refused them access, so they settled instead in the neighboring country of Burma (today's Myanmar). That country would never be the same again.

At the time of the Judsons' arrival, there wasn't a single Christian in Burma. They labored for six long years before they met Moung Nau and led him to Christ. After the baptism, Judson wrote in his journal, "Oh, may it prove to be the beginning of a series of baptisms in the Burman empire which shall continue in uninterrupted success to the end of the age."

That prayer was answered over time. Slowly but surely, the kingdom of God began to grow in Burma. But along with success came tragedy and persecution. The couple lost two children on the mission field. To make matters even worse, Judson was arrested and charged with being a British spy. The stress of his twenty-one-month imprisonment took its toll on his wife, Ann, and she also died on the mission field, as would Judson's second wife, Sarah Hall.

When Adoniram Judson finally died at the age of sixty-two, he'd spent thirty-eight years ministering in Burma. The suffering he endured was almost unfathomable. . .but so was the fruit he bore for God's kingdom. Soon after his death, the Burmese government reported that there were 210,000 Christians living in the land. . .one out of every fifty-eight Burmese!

Fanny J. Crosby

Have you ever met a blind person who influenced thousands of churches (and millions of Christians, by extension), as well as presidents and members of Congress? If not, it's because you never met Fanny J. Crosby.

Crosby was born in 1820 with the ability to see, but within

two months she had lost her eyesight because of a quack doctor's malpractice. A few months later, she also lost her father. Crosby's mother couldn't afford the expenses of raising a blind child, so the young girl was raised by her grandmother, a devout Christian.

At the age of fifteen, Crosby was sent to the New York Institute for the Blind, where she began to write poetry and music. When a visiting phrenologist saw her work, he encouraged her to explore her gifts. "Here is a poetess. Give her every possible encouragement. . . . You will hear from this young lady someday."

In fact, the whole world would hear from that young lady.

In her lifetime, Fanny Crosby authored more than nine thousand hymns, including "Safe in the Arms of Jesus," "Blessed Assurance," "To God Be the Glory," "Pass Me Not, O Gentle Savior," and "Jesus Keep Me Near the Cross." She knew and influenced all six presidents who served during her lifetime and made multiple addresses to Congress. Her work has outlived her by many generations. Not a Sunday goes by that her hymns aren't sung in churches around the world.

These world changers had one thing in common: the Holy Spirit dwelling within them. The Holy Spirit lived in them to help them serve God—*sometimes in the face of fierce opposition*—so others could know Jesus and glorify Him.

That's how Jesus describes the Holy Spirit's work in Acts 1:8:

You will receive power when the Holy Spirit comes on you; and you will be my witnesses in

Jerusalem, and in all Judea and Samaria, and to
the ends of the earth.

The Holy Spirit empowered the first apostles, in the book of Acts, to serve God, glorify Jesus, and change the world. And He has continued His work down through the ages. He wants to empower *you* to do the same, starting now!

Opening

1. Of the four people discussed above—William Carey, Martha Myers, Adoniram Judson, and Fanny Crosby—who do you think did the most exciting and influential work? Why?

2. In what way(s) did the Holy Spirit empower each of these heroes of the faith to serve God and bring glory to Jesus?

3. For what reason, according to Acts 1:8, did Jesus say the Holy Spirit would empower believers. . .and what does that mean?

4. Do you think the Holy Spirit still works in the lives of believers today, empowering them to serve God and bringing glory to Jesus? Why or why not?

Bible Passage

Acts 4:1–21

This story takes place on the heels of a great miracle performed by Peter and John (through the power of the Holy Spirit, of course). In Acts 3, the two apostles meet a beggar who has been disabled since birth, and they heal him in the name of Jesus. This creates a citywide buzz and gives Peter an opportunity to talk about Jesus even more. But the actions of the apostles put them on a collision course with the rulers of the day.

> *The priests and the captain of the temple guard and the Sadducees came up to Peter and John while they were speaking to the people. They were greatly disturbed because the apostles were teaching the people, proclaiming in Jesus the resurrection of the dead. They seized Peter and John, and because it was evening, they put them in jail until the next day. But many who heard the message believed; so the number of men who believed grew to about five thousand.*
>
> *The next day the rulers, the elders and the teachers of the law met in Jerusalem. Annas the high priest was there, and so were Caiaphas, John, Alexander and others of the high priest's family. They had Peter and John brought before them and began to question them: "By what power or what name did you do this?"*

Then Peter, filled with the Holy Spirit, said to them: "Rulers and elders of the people! If we are being called to account today for an act of kindness shown to a man who was lame and are being asked how he was healed, then know this, you and all the people of Israel: It is by the name of Jesus Christ of Nazareth, whom you crucified but whom God raised from the dead, that this man stands before you healed. Jesus is "the stone you builders rejected, which has become the cornerstone.' Salvation is found in no one else, for there is no other name under heaven given to mankind by which we must be saved."

When they saw the courage of Peter and John and realized that they were unschooled, ordinary men, they were astonished and they took note that these men had been with Jesus. But since they could see the man who had been healed standing there with them, there was nothing they could say. So they ordered them to withdraw from the Sanhedrin and then conferred together. "What are we going to do with these men?" they asked. "Everybody living in Jerusalem knows they have performed a notable sign, and we cannot deny it. But to stop this thing from spreading any further among the people, we must warn them to speak no longer to anyone in this name."

Then they called them in again and

commanded them not to speak or teach at all in
the name of Jesus. But Peter and John replied,
"Which is right in God's eyes: to listen to you, or to
him? You be the judges! As for us, we cannot help
speaking about what we have seen and heard."

After further threats they let them go. They
could not decide how to punish them, because all the
people were praising God for what had happened.

Study Questions

1. How did the Holy Spirit empower Peter and John to serve God, and how did that glorify Jesus?

2. William Carey, Martha Myers, Adoniram Judson, and Fanny Crosby overcame significant obstacles to serve God. In this passage, what obstacles did the Holy Spirit enable Peter and John to overcome so they could serve God and glorify Jesus?

3. When Carey, Myers, Judson, and Crosby served God in the power of the Holy Spirit, the world around them was changed. What changed in and around Jerusalem when the Holy Spirit filled Peter and John? (Read the passage closely; there are several indicators of big changes.)

4. From the passage, it's clear that Peter and John fully relied on the power of the Holy Spirit to serve God. Why do we so often rely on our own power to try to serve God?

Deeper Questions

1. In a huge study of American Christians—adults who were self-professed believers—researchers discovered that 58 percent (more than half) thought the Holy Spirit was "a symbol of God's power or presence, but is not a living entity." Why are so many Christians confused about the identity of the Holy Spirit? What effect does that misunderstanding have on their spiritual lives?

2. We have access to the same Holy Spirit that Peter and John had access to (along with Carey, Myers, Judson, Crosby, and many more). So why are millions of Christians powerless and ineffective in their service to God?

3. God used people like Peter and John in remarkable ways, even though they were described as "unschooled, ordinary men." What does that say about the potential for God using you?

Application Questions

1. Have you identified any spiritual gifts the Holy Spirit has given you? If so, what are they? If not, do you have a plan to discover them?

2. Since the Holy Spirit is a person. . .name two ways you can begin personally interacting with Him right away.

3. How does God want you to start serving Him immediately. . .and how can the Holy Spirit help you?

Final Word

For years, Nick Lappos was on the front line of production at the Sikorsky Aircraft Corporation, the company that created some of the most incredible machines ever to take flight, including the massive Jolly Green Giant and the world-renowned Blackhawk helicopter. Lappos served in various capacities during his career, most notably as the Chief R&D test pilot for his company's inventions. When Sikorsky produced the RAH-66, more commonly known as the Comanche, Lappos sat in the cockpit to test one of the most lethal aircrafts ever to soar in the sky.

At the time, the Comanche was unlike any other helicopter in the world. It incorporated radar-absorbent material and had a highly decreased noise signature that pushed it into a completely different realm of stealth capability. It also had advanced navigation and enemy detection systems to allow pilots to be the first to strike in a fight. And when that strike came, it happened on the business end of a three-barreled 20mm cannon, Hellfire rockets, and Stinger missiles.

To put it bluntly, when the Comanche took flight, it took control of the skies. The dominance of the Comanche against air-to-air and air-to-ground targets was so drastic that it caused Lappos to famously state, "If you find yourself in a fair fight, you didn't plan it properly."

If you choose to follow Jesus, you will be engaging in the most *unfair* fight of your life. There's simply no way you can stand up alone to the challenges and outright opposition of our enemy Satan. Every disciple who's intent on following Jesus will be confronted by the devil's attempts to thwart us from bringing glory to God's Son.

That's one of the major reasons God gave us the Holy Spirit: to give us the upper hand in that battle. *The Holy Spirit is the power of God in our lives.* When the apostle John realized how mighty the Holy Spirit was, he wrote the following line to his friends who were serving God alongside him:

> *You, dear children, are from God and have overcome them, because the one who is in you is greater than the one who is in the world. (1 John 4:4)*

The Holy Spirit doesn't make our fight *fair;* He tips the balance so far in our favor that we can confidently serve God knowing that victory has already been assured. So, if you find yourself losing an unfair fight, it's because you're living without the power of the Holy Spirit in your life. Do yourself a favor and don't try to follow Jesus without the help, leadership, and power of the Holy Spirit in your life.

It won't be pretty.

There wasn't anything inherently special about Peter and John (or any person in the Bible, for that matter). In fact, Luke, the writer of Acts, quotes the religious leaders as calling the two men "unschooled" and "ordinary." But God's Spirit lived in them and empowered them in mighty ways because their lives were focused on what the Holy Spirit is focused on: *glorifying Jesus.*

Here's the really exciting part: *The Holy Spirit wants to do the same work through you.*

No matter what some theologians may tell you, the Holy

Spirit is just as much alive today as He was in the book of Acts. Didn't the Holy Spirit help the likes of William Carey, Martha Myers, Adoniram Judson, and Fanny Crosby? And the Holy Spirit still has the same supernatural power He displayed back then, as well. The Holy Spirit is constantly searching for people whom He can fill so they can then be poured out for Jesus.

It's truly sad that so many Christians are deeply confused about the Holy Spirit's identity and work. In reality, those who are confused about the Holy Spirit are confused about none other than God Himself.

You don't have to be one of them.

Ask the Holy Spirit to fill you, live within you, and help you serve God boldly so that Jesus can be glorified in your life. You'll never be the same again.

5

Sin and Salvation

Which do you want first, the Good News. . .or the bad news?

On September 28, 2011, Michael Cohen made a decision that changed his life.

The middle-aged British man, who lived in South Africa, wanted to go for a swim in the beautiful waters of the Atlantic Ocean near Cape Town. *Who wouldn't?* The beaches in Cape Town are gorgeous; you can stroll along the shore, catch a tan on the sand, or jump into the cool waters for a swim.

That is, unless the great whites are patrolling *their* side of the shoreline.

It's not unusual for the behemoth predators to swim in the shallow waters off the coast of Cape Town; in fact, they're so abundant in that region that entire documentaries are filmed there. (You've probably seen footage of the huge sharks breaching the surface high into the air in pursuit of those slippery seals.) Shark sightings are so frequent in Cape Town that the city developed a "shark spotter" program to help keep beachgoers safe.

On that fateful morning, at least three great white sharks had been seen by the helicopter-assisted lifeguards. The city's employees followed standard operating procedures at that point: raising warning flags along the shore and closing the beach.

Most people took the hint. But despite all the warnings, Michael Cohen went into the water for a swim. Did he not see the flags? Were there no lifeguards around to stop him? Sadly, no. He saw (and heard) all the warnings and was even told by lifeguards—*repeatedly*—to stay out of the water. But he went in, anyway.

He never stood a chance.

As the lone swimmer in the water at the time, Cohen made an easy target for the prowling whites. Eyewitnesses claimed the massive sharks lunged at him in savage brutality, using their razor-sharp teeth to bite off his right leg at the knee and badly mangle his left leg. Those same eyewitnesses watched Cohen helplessly flail his arms in the bloody water as Mother Nature's perfect predator moved in for the kill.[3]

Those who witnessed the attack and those who read about it later were left to ponder one very simple question: *Why did he break the rules and get in the water?*

It's easy to sit in judgment of people like Michael Cohen. *That was stupid! What a fool! Did he have a death wish, or something? What was he thinking? Why would he ignore repeated warnings from multiple lifeguards just so he could do his own thing?*

But everyone who points an accusatory finger at Michael

Cohen's foolish actions is left to answer a similar question: *Why do we so often ignore God so we can do our own thing?*

I Have Some Bad News. . .

I hope you're sitting down, because I have some (really) bad news: you and I act even more foolishly than Michael Cohen, and we face much more devastating consequences as a result of our stupidity.

Oh, and we do it every single day.

I know that sounds inflammatory, and maybe even insulting. But do yourself a favor and read just a few more paragraphs before you decide.

The Bible, which we've already learned in chapter 2 tells the truth about God, us, and life, has some rather scathing descriptions of you and me: Scripture calls us *sinners.* Here are just three simple examples of that harsh reality:

- *All have turned away, all have become corrupt; there is no one who does good, not even one. (Psalm 14:3)*

- *All of us have become like one who is unclean, and all our righteous acts are like filthy rags; we all shrivel up like a leaf, and like the wind our sins sweep us away. (Isaiah 64:6)*

- *All have sinned and fall short of the glory of God. (Romans 3:23)*

In case you think you're exempt for some reason, go back and look at the very first word of those three verses. Yep, "all." That includes you.

So, what's a sinner? What does that mean?

In short, sin is the breaking of God's law. One theologian describes sin as "cosmic rebellion against God." For example, God's words command us not to lie to one another (Colossians 3:9), yet research conducted by Drs. Kim Serota, Timothy Levine, and Franklin Boster found that most of us tell 1.65 lies every single day.

We're all a bunch of big, fat Pinocchios! (And sinners.)

God's words also tell us to steer clear of stealing (Exodus 20:15). Pretty basic, right? Don't take stuff that doesn't belong to you. We were taught that simple lesson as children, and if you have children, you've no doubt tried to teach it to them, as well. But here's the problem: 45 percent of Americans admit to "pirating" copyrighted media (for example, illegally downloading a song or copying a friend's Blu-ray). We call it "being tech savvy" or "no big deal" to make ourselves feel better.

God's words call it theft. (And sin.)

Let's cover one more really quickly. In Proverbs 6:25, God warns us to avoid lust. Jesus, in His first public teaching, does the same thing (Matthew 5:27–28). When we give our eyes, our attention, and our desires over to lust, it can consume us, destroy us, and ruin marriages and families; bad stuff all around. Yet 70 percent of men and 30 percent of women admit to watching pornography. In fact, porn sites are visited more often than Netflix, Amazon, and Twitter combined! And do we even need to discuss sexting (the sending and receiving of provocative or nude pictures)? We all know teens do it, but a growing number of adults do it, as well. Even politicians do it!

Looks like we're all a bunch of perverts (and sinners!).

You might be thinking, *I've never lied, lifted, or lusted in my life.* Great! But we could keep going. There's greed (Luke 12:15), laziness (Hebrews 6:12), envy (Exodus 20:17), idolatry (1 Corinthians 10:14), and disobedience to parents (Colossians 3:20).

I'm pretty sure one of those describes you. Like me, your grandma, the pope, and Hitler, you're a dirty rotten low-down scoundrel of a sinner.

I know that's bad news. . .and it's about to get worse.

There's Nothing You Can Do about It

You've probably never wondered why you have the color eyes you have. That's because you already know the answer: *You were born with them.* Likewise, it doesn't require much thought for you to understand why you have the color hair you have. *You were born with it.* But you might be wondering why the Bible calls you a sinner. The answer is just as simple as your eye color and hair color: *You were born that way.*

To get a firm grasp on our common human problem, we have to go back to the very beginning of history. The Bible records this part of our saga in Genesis 1–3, the first three chapters of God's words. You're probably somewhat familiar with the story, but a brief reminder might be helpful.

In the beginning, there was just God—which, as we've

seen, includes Father, Son, and Holy Spirit. Then God created a man and gave him the name Adam. And because God really loved Adam, He created a woman for him, named Eve. God gave the two newly crafted humans free reign over a paradise called the Garden of Eden and put them in charge of taking care of it. Then God gave them a single rule: Don't eat the fruit from one particular tree. All the other trees are fine, but not this one. Simple enough, right? Don't eat the fruit from this *one* tree. . .or you'll die.

Kinda like, "Don't go into shark-infested waters. . .or you will die."

But guess what they did? Yep, they chose to disregard God's warning and ate from the tree anyway. And just as God had said, their disobedience brought death into the world. For starters, the woman would thereafter struggle with painful childbirth, and the man would forever struggle with toilsome work, growing crops from the ground until he died and returned to the ground himself. Then God evicted them from the Garden of Eden. They were tossed out of the garden—and out of God's presence—because they had rebelled against God. And, finally, we're told the saddest news of all: Both Adam and Eve eventually died.

None of those consequences—brokenness, separation, and death—was part of God's plan for Adam and Eve. But sin wasn't God's plan for them, either. They had become sinners, and every generation since have been sinners as well.

Yep. We are born sinners.

For every single one of us, sin is a part of our nature because it's *embedded* in us from birth. Think about it. Did your parents have to teach you to lie? Nope, you knew that one all on your own. In fact, they had to teach you to tell the truth. Did anyone have to explain greed to you when you were a child? Again, no. *Mine* is one of the first words we all learn. We are sinners because sin is *in* us.

Our sin nature also explains why sinning comes to us so *naturally*. We don't have to try to sin; it's not like we have to warm up or stretch before we start sinning. Sadly, we can sin at a moment's notice. That's because it is our *nature* to sin.

Sin Nature

Our nature describes what we are like; for example, outgoing or shy, analytical or emotional, and so on. Our nature is the makeup of who we are; unfortunately, our nature as humans is sinful. Because we are the offspring of the original sinners, Adam and Eve, we've inherited their tendency to sin. Our default setting in life is to sin. When someone hurts us, our gut reaction is to seek revenge. We routinely give in to jealousy, gossip, addictions, and much more. Two thousand years ago, the apostle Paul, one of the best men who ever lived, described his own sin nature in Romans 7:15–21. It wasn't pretty.

This entire book hinges on the unique beliefs that Christians hold, but it's interesting to note that, on the point of human brokenness, every major world religion agrees with Christianity. People of every faith—*and people of no faith*—can see that *something* is wrong with us. Humans murder, rape, steal, lie, and cheat. Nobody denies that reality. Granted, different people may use different terms to describe what's wrong with us, but the harsh reality remains: We are broken, badly broken.

Even though the major world religions agree that we are sinful creatures, we strongly disagree on the best way to deal with our sin. On numerous occasions, I've been invited to speak on behalf of Christianity as part of a panel or debate with leaders of other religions. Inevitably, we are asked the same question (in some form or other): *How do we fix what's wrong with us?*

Some religious leaders start off by talking about balancing our good deeds with our bad deeds. It's a highly popular idea because it appeals to our sense of fairness; after all, certain criminals are given community service sentences to offset their crimes. They've hurt their community by breaking the law, so they must do something good to help their community. There's just one problem: How do we know when we've done enough good to offset the bad?

How many little old ladies do I have to walk across the street to balance out murder?

Other spiritual leaders (and psychologists) talk about the strategy of forgiving ourselves. It's quite a popular trend; in fact, this idea has crept into some of today's most-celebrated media. For example, in Linkin Park's wildly popular song *What I've Done* (which rose to the Top 10 on *Billboard*'s Hot 100 and served as the theme song for the movie *Transformers*), the band wrestles with the brokenness of humanity that they see in the world. . .*and in themselves.* They lament that humanity's sins are ruining the planet as well as our species. They know they are guilty, as well, so they hatch a plan to solve their problem—

essentially creating their own clean slate: "I start again and whatever pain may come. . .I'm forgiving what I've done."

Sorry, guys, but sin can't be overcome that way.

If it could, even the vilest offenders—people like Hitler, Stalin, and Bin Laden—and millions of others, like you and me, could simply say, "My bad," and be excused.

We have to remember that *we* aren't the only ones affected by our sin. Sin has a negative impact on everyone around us, as well. Stealing hurts others. Lying wounds others. Adultery certainly destroys others. Don't we need the forgiveness of those we've hurt and offended? And what about God? The Bible teaches that He, too, is offended by our sin.

Of course, lots of people try to blame others for their sins. If they can shift the responsibility of their actions onto others, they feel justified or excused. This is literally the oldest trick in the book; if you look at the very first sin ever committed in human history, the sin of Adam and Eve, you'll see this strategy in play. Check out what Adam says when God busts him in the Garden of Eden:

> *The man said, "The woman you put here with me—she gave me some fruit from the tree, and I ate it." (Genesis 3:12)*

What a great guy, huh? *"It was all her fault, God! She's the one who made me do it!"* I don't know about you, but that line didn't work with my parents; I don't think it will work with God, either. In fact, anybody who can read can see it didn't work with God.

I can't, in good conscience, recommend any of those strategies for dealing with sin. They simply don't work. So, what can we do to fix our sin problem?

According to the Bible, nothing.

There is absolutely nothing we can do to erase or alleviate our sin. We're all sinners, and there is nothing we can do about it. I know that's some awful news, but it's about to get a whole lot worse.

The Worst News of All

Umm. . .if you weren't seated before, you may want to sit down for this next part.

Your sin deserves death. *Your death.* No matter how large or small your sin was, no matter how recent or long ago it happened, and no matter if it was public or private, your sin demands your death.

Death is the only fitting conclusion, according to the Bible. Listen to what God said about our sin in James 1:15:

> *After desire has conceived, it gives birth to sin;*
> *and sin, when it is full-grown, gives birth to death.*

In other words, our desire (sinful cravings) leads to sin, and sin (the breaking of God's law) leads to death. The Bible even includes a few harrowing examples of this principle in its pages. Here is the short version of just a few of them.

David and Bathsheba

This is really the go-to story for showing the fierce consequences of our sin. King David was Israel's favorite king. He was handsome (which never hurts), he killed a giant (which was really cool), and he improved his nation's political and spiritual health. An all-around great guy.

One evening, while King David was walking around the ramparts of his palace, he saw a naked woman bathing a few houses down the street. The woman wasn't just any woman; she was the wife of Uriah, one of David's best friends and most capable warriors. But in this moment none of that meant anything to David, so he took Bathsheba into his chambers and slept with her. . .and she became pregnant.

Now David had a real problem on his hands. He tried to cover up his sin by bringing Uriah home from war to sleep with Bathsheba, but that didn't work. (Uriah wouldn't think of sleeping in his own bed when his comrades in arms were sleeping in tents in faraway fields. Instead, he humbly slept on the palace floor.) In the end, David sent a letter to the commander of the army instructing him to make sure that Uriah—his dear friend—was killed in battle. Not long after Uriah's death, Bathsheba gave birth to a son, but he died a few days later. You can read the full account of this awful sin in 2 Samuel 11, but know this: David sinned. . . and two others died. (By the way, this wasn't the only time David sinned and others lost their lives. The scariest story in the Bible can be found in 2 Samuel 24.) *Sin always leads to death.*

Ananias and Sapphira

Jump forward to the New Testament for another terrifying example. A husband and wife named Ananias and Sapphira were members of the early church. Like many people, they wanted other people to think highly of them. The only problem was that these two were willing to perpetrate an elaborate hoax in order to gain admiration.

It went down like this: A disciple named Barnabas sold some property and made a large donation to the church. He didn't do it for the praise of others, but Ananias and Sapphira saw an opportunity to elevate themselves by mimicking him... sort of. The couple also went and sold some property, but instead of giving 100 percent of the proceeds to the church, they kept back some of the money and just *claimed* it was 100 percent of the sale price.

This deceitful act of jealousy and manipulation angered God so much that He struck both of them dead to set an example for all the other true believers. You can read the story in Acts 5, but again, just know going in: *sin always leads to death*.

Just to recap so far: You and I are sinners. There is nothing we can do about it. And our sin leads to death.

I don't know about you, but I'm about ready for some good news.

Rescued

When we last considered Michael Cohen, blood was pouring from his shark-inflicted wounds, leaving him weak and in grave danger. Having that much blood in the water isn't a good thing, for two reasons: First, the blood isn't *in your body* where it belongs, and second, it's attracting other sharks. There was absolutely no way that Michael Cohen was going to make it back to shore on his own. He was as good as dead.

Enter Douglas Drysdale and Hugh Till, two average guys who regularly volunteered at the local prison to encourage the inmates to adopt a life a faith. As they left the prison that day, they drove along the elevated coastal road looking for whales. But as they neared the Fish Hoek beach, what they saw caused them to step out—*or swim out*—in faith.

At first, they saw the warning signs and the solitary swimmer out in the surf. And then they saw the sharks. Hastily parking their car, they ran down to the beach to warn the man who was out in the water. But it was too late.

As they arrived on the beach, they saw Michael Cohen struggling against the waves, they saw blood in the water, and of course, they saw the ruthless predators still circling their prey. Without hesitation, Drysdale and Till kicked off their shoes and ran toward the crashing waves. Plunging into the blood-tinged water, they swam out toward the sharks and pulled the dying man back to the shoreline. As soon as they hit the sand, several bystanders fashioned a tourniquet from two belts and a wetsuit and kept Cohen alive until he could be airlifted by helicopter to the local hospital.[3]

I can only imagine the hope and relief Michael Cohen felt when Douglas Drysdale and Hugh Till began tugging him toward the shoreline. Given the chaos of the moment and the fact that, when they woke up that morning, they (probably) hadn't planned to rescue anyone from shark-infested waters, their rescue plan may have looked something like this:

1. Swim out to sea.
2. Grab the idiot.
3. Get back alive.

I don't know for sure. I'm just guessing. I've never rescued anyone from shark-infested waters.

Michael Cohen survived his unnecessarily traumatic experience and eventually recovered to the point where he could be released from the hospital. But to this day, his body still bears the scars that are evidence of his disobedience. Make no mistake: like Michael Cohen, we've all broken the law with our sin. Like Michael Cohen, we've all done irreparable harm through our sin. Like Michael Cohen, we've all jeopardized our very lives because of our sin.

And as with Michael Cohen, a rescuer has come to save us.

A Strange Way to Save the World

Jesus is that rescuer. . .but He used one of the strangest rescue plans ever devised.

Unlike the rescue plan of Hugh Till and Douglas Drysdale, we know *exactly* what Jesus' rescue plan looked like, mainly because He described it (several times) before He enacted it. Listen to what Jesus says about Himself, the Son of Man, and

His plan to rescue the world from its sin:

> *Jesus took the Twelve aside and told them, "We are going up to Jerusalem, and everything that is written by the prophets about the Son of Man will be fulfilled. He will be delivered over to the Gentiles. They will mock him, insult him and spit on him; they will flog him and kill him. On the third day he will rise again." Luke 18:31–33)*

Umm. . .that's a lot different from the rescue plans we've seen in the movies. No diversions. No stealthy surprise. Not a single explosion. Jesus basically said, "Listen up fellas. This is how it's gonna go down. I'm gonna bust in. . .*and die*. . .after being mocked, insulted, spit on, and flogged, of course."

Bruce Willis never did it that way. . . .

Jesus said that His plan would be in accordance with what had been written by the prophets centuries earlier. Look at how one of those prophets describes the plan Jesus would follow to rescue us from sin:

> *He was pierced for our transgressions, he was crushed for our iniquities; the punishment that brought us peace was upon him, and by his wounds we are healed. We all, like sheep, have gone astray, each of us has turned to our own way; and the LORD has laid on him the iniquity of us all.*

*He was oppressed and afflicted, yet he did
not open his mouth; he was led like a lamb to
the slaughter, and as a sheep before its shearers is
silent, so he did not open his mouth. By oppression
and judgment he was taken away. Yet who of
his generation protested? For he was cut off from
the land of the living; for the transgression of my
people he was punished. (Isaiah 53:5–8)*

Jesus' plan to save us hinged on His death. Though it might not *sound* like a rescue plan, it was actually quite perfect. To rescue us from our sin, Jesus Christ, the perfect Son of God, willingly and sacrificially gave His life on the cross—*dying in our rightful place*—to pay the price of our sin and restore our relationship with a holy and perfect God. The Bible calls this *salvation*, and it's only possible through the gracious act of Jesus' death on our behalf.

Salvation

This is one of the easiest theological concepts to explain. Salvation is simply the act of being saved. The Bible is filled with examples of God saving His people, and they always have two common characteristics: first, the act of salvation is miraculous in nature; and second, it is done by God Himself. God saved the Israelites at the Red Sea (Exodus 14:1-31); He saved Shadrach, Meshach, and Abednego from the fiery furnace (Daniel 3:1-30); and He saved Jonah from a whale (Jonah 2:1-10). Of course, the greatest example of God's salvation was when He saved us from our sin through Jesus. There's no other salvation like that!

The salvation Jesus offers us is more than just a rescue from death. It's more than just a rescue from the shame and guilt of our past, too. In fact, it's even more than just a rescue from eternal separation from God in hell. (We'll talk more about that in chapter 7.) The salvation Jesus gives to us is also a rescue from our sin nature. Listen to how Paul describes his sin nature (and see if you can relate). Don't miss how he says he was rescued from it.

> I know that good itself does not dwell in me, that is, in my sinful nature. For I have the desire to do what is good, but I cannot carry it out. For I do not do the good I want to do, but the evil I do not want to do—this I keep on doing. Now if I do what I do not want to do, it is no longer I who do it, but it is sin living in me that does it. So I find this law at work: Although I want to do good, evil is right there with me. For in my inner being I delight in God's law; but I see another law at work in me, waging war against the law of my mind and making me a prisoner of the law of sin at work within me. What a wretched man I am! Who will rescue me from this body that is subject to death? Thanks be to God, who delivers me through Jesus Christ our Lord! (Romans 7:18–25)

A major part of God's salvation for us through Jesus, Paul says, was so that we could finally overcome our sin nature. We don't have to be our old selves anymore. Through Jesus, we are free to live completely new lives.

Salvation through Jesus was God's idea for us all along. In fact, all the way back in the Garden of Eden when He was dealing with the sin of Adam and Eve (Genesis 3:15), God hints at the salvation that only Jesus can bring. In chapter 1, not only did we discover some great reasons for believing that God exists, we also found out that He's best described as perfect love. God loves us so much that He sent His only perfect Son, Jesus, to die for us. At least, that's what one of the Bible's best-known verses says:

> *For God so loved the world that he gave his one and only Son, that whoever believes in him shall not perish but have eternal life. (John 3:16)*

Though God is gracious for granting us salvation—*miraculously and personally rescuing us from our sin*—He is adamant about how it happens: salvation comes only through His Son, Jesus. That makes sense, when you think about sin. For sin to be forgiven, a perfect sacrifice had to be made. Because Jesus was the *only* person ever to live a perfect and sinless life, He is the only one whose death could pay for our sins. In other words, nobody else's death can save you, because they're in the same boat you are. . .the *USS Sinner*.

The Gospel

The Gospel is literally the "Good News" that Jesus has come to save us from our sin. We were once alienated from God, living as His enemies, and facing the penalty of death and eternal separation from Him. That's really bad news. But when Jesus came to Earth, died on the cross, and rose from the dead, He did so to pay the price (in full) for our sins, set us free from bondage, and reconcile us to God. That is the Gospel, the ultimate Good News.

Strangely, there are lots of people who have a problem with that reality. They don't like the fact that *only* Jesus can save them. Maybe they think Jesus is too controversial. Others may feel He is too weak. (He did die, after all.) Some don't trust Him; and, for many, Jesus just isn't their type.

Can you imagine Michael Cohen saying that to his two rescuers? *"Nah, I don't think I want you guys to save me. You're too tall. You're too hairy. You're fans of a rival football team. Thanks, but no thanks. I'll wait for someone else to come along."*

Michael Cohen knew only one thing about his rescuers: they were willing to risk their lives to save his. . .and that was enough for him to trust them.

If you know only one thing about Jesus, let it be this: he willingly took the punishment for your sins so you wouldn't have to. That's wild, reckless, and unselfish love. That's the Gospel!

Without a doubt, the focal point of the entire Bible is the life of Jesus Christ—specifically, His death and resurrection. The entire Old Testament points to His coming, and the entire New Testament talks about what He did when He got here. Jesus accomplished many things, but His chief objective on earth was offering us salvation from our sins by dying on the cross and being raised from the dead three days later.

Here's the Good News, in case somehow you missed it: *You* can be rescued by Jesus. . .*if* you put your trust in Him alone. But He won't just save you *from* your sins; He'll save you *for* a life-changing purpose, as well. We'll look at that purpose in the next few chapters.

Session 5

Sin and Salvation

Which do you want first, the Good News. . .or the bad news?

Big Idea: We need to be rescued from sin, but we cannot save ourselves. Jesus is our only hope.

Passage: Ephesians 2:1–9

Discussion Starter: *Hap Halloran: Rescuing Ray*

Born in 1922, Ray Halloran grew up in Cincinnati and volunteered for the Army Air Forces shortly after the attack on Pearl Harbor in 1941. During his training stateside, Halloran became proficient as a navigator and bombardier on the newly designed B-29 bomber. Ray's happy-go-lucky attitude earned him the nickname "Hap" by members of his flight crew, known as the Rover Boys Express, all of whom were deployed to the island of Saipan when their training was complete.

On January 27, 1945, during their fourth mission over the Japanese mainland, Hap's B-29 was engaged by a twin-engine

Japanese fighter plane and riddled with bullets over the northeast edge of Tokyo. The crew members who were still alive were promptly ordered to jump out of the doomed aircraft. Hap and the survivors bailed out into the chaotic skies. . . which were a bone-chilling minus fifty-eight degrees. After free-falling from 27,000 feet, Hap deployed his chute and descended into enemy territory. He was immediately taken prisoner by Japanese civilians, who brutally beat him before turning him over to the authorities.

By nightfall, Hap was on a truck headed to the Kempeitai (military police) torture prison in downtown Tokyo near the Imperial Palace. For more than two months, he was placed in solitary confinement in a cold, dark cage in a wooden stable and was subjected to forced starvation and repeated attacks by the Japanese guards. During his stay, he received very little food and no medical treatment for his injuries. Any prisoner who broke the rule of absolute silence faced death. Sadly, Hap witnessed more than one execution of POWs who were caught talking.

Eventually, Hap was removed from his wooden cage and taken to Ueno Zoo in downtown Tokyo where he was stripped of all his clothes and put on display in a tiger cage for civilians to walk by and taunt. By this time, he'd lost eighty pounds and his filthy body was covered with running sores from bed bugs, fleas, and lice infestations. The only solace Hap found from the extremely barbaric conditions was in prayer.

Finally, Hap was moved to the Omori prisoner of war

facility on the southwest side of Tokyo. But since the Japanese refused to identify the building as a POW building, Hap and the other prisoners suffered under daily barrages by US bombers who didn't know that fellow airmen were suffering underneath their bombs. It was a grueling four months at the Omori facility, but it was here that Hap experienced the most significant moment in his life.

On August 29, 1945, US Marines crashed through the gates of the prison, setting Hap and the other POWs free from their brutal suffering. Hap was taken aboard the hospital ship *Benevolence*, floating in Tokyo Bay and was able to take his first bath in months. He also consumed eighteen Milky Way candy bars.

On August 28, 1945, Ray Halloran was a prisoner who could not save himself. One day later, he was set free because he had been rescued by someone else. He had been saved. Someone did something for Hap that he could not do for himself.

Opening Questions

1. Of all that Hap suffered, which torture was the worst in your opinion? Why?

2. Why couldn't Hap just save himself from the POW camp?

3. Put yourself in Hap's shoes. What would you have felt when you saw those Marines busting down the gates to set you free after so long?

4. How was Hap's captivity in the POW camp like our imprisonment to our sin nature?

5. Hap needed salvation from a POW camp; we need salvation from our sin. What is salvation, and why is it so important?

Bible Passage
Ephesians 2:1–9

> *As for you, you were dead in your transgressions and sins, in which you used to live when you followed the ways of this world and of the ruler of the kingdom of the air, the spirit who is now at work in those who are disobedient. All of us also lived among them at one time, gratifying the cravings of our flesh and following its desires and thoughts. Like the rest, we were by nature deserving of wrath. But because of his great love for us, God, who is rich in mercy, made us alive with Christ even when we were dead in transgressions—it is by grace you have been saved. And God raised us up with Christ and seated us with him in the heavenly realms in Christ Jesus, in order that in the coming ages he might show the incomparable riches of his grace, expressed in his kindness to us in Christ Jesus. For it is by grace you have been saved, through faith—and this not from yourselves, it is the gift of God—not by works, so that no one can boast.*

Study Questions

1. What is the grim picture Paul uses in verse 1 to describe our predicament?

2. According to Paul, what are the attributes of God that prompted Him to act on our behalf?

3. Though Paul says we were "dead in our transgressions and sins," what does he say God has done for us?

4. Is God's punishment for our sin—*death*— too harsh? Why or why not?

5. Paul tells us—*twice*—that we are saved by grace. What is grace?

6. Have you ever tried to save yourself from your sin? If so, what happened as a result?

Deeper Questions

1. Take a look at the explanation behind finding a worm *inside* an apple (from http://itslikethis.org/?p=1785). How is this like our sin nature that Paul writes about in Ephesians 2:3?

2. Take a look at the *kristos* in the Philippines (from http://itslikethis.org/?p=48). It's an

extreme example of people trying to offset their sins, for sure! But why won't it work, according to the Bible?

3. The Bible emphatically teaches that Jesus is the only source of salvation. Jesus even said it Himself in John 14:6: *"I am the way and the truth and the life. No one comes to the Father except through me."* But many people reject Jesus and His salvation, in spite of His sacrifice. How do you think it makes God the Father feel knowing He sent His only Son to die for people who would reject Him?

Application Questions

1. How has Jesus allowed you to overcome your sin nature since He rescued you? In other words, how is your life different now that Jesus has saved you from your sin?

2. In what ways can you live out your gratitude to Jesus for being the one who rescued you from your sins?

Final Word

Michael Cohen couldn't save himself from the sharks. He needed to be rescued. Hap Halloran also needed a rescuer because he couldn't save himself from the POW camp. Like those two men, you and I are in a life-and-death predicament of sin, from which we cannot save ourselves. Like them, our only hope is to be rescued.

The clearest message in the Bible is this: *Jesus is our rescuer.* The story of our sin (the bad news) and God's salvation (the Good News) can be told as a story of two trees. The first tree grew in the Garden of Eden, and on it hung fruit that God had forbidden Adam and Eve to eat.

> *The LORD God commanded the man, "You are free to eat from any tree in the garden; but you must not eat from the tree of the knowledge of good and evil, for when you eat from it you will certainly die." (Genesis 2:16–17)*

When it came to that particular tree, Adam and Eve didn't obey God. Instead, they ate from the tree. . .*and they died.* When you and I disobey God, we suffer the same consequences.

But there was a second tree. No fruit hung on this tree; instead, a Savior hung on it. Listen to how Peter described the cross—the *tree*—on which Jesus hung for our sin:

> *He [Jesus] committed no sin, and no deceit was found in his mouth. When they hurled their insults at him, he did not retaliate; when he suffered, he made no threats. Instead, he entrusted himself to him who judges justly. "He himself bore our sins" in his body on the cross, so that we might die to sins and live for righteousness; "by his wounds you have been healed." (1 Peter 2:22–24)*

Unlike Adam and Eve, Jesus *obeyed* God about His tree; Jesus "entrusted Himself to Him who judges justly." He suffered greatly, not just through insults and wounds, but under *our* sin, as well. Ultimately, Jesus died on *His* tree to give us life after we lost it on *our* tree.

The first tree led to tragedy. The second led to triumph.

We sinned against God, and that sin cost us everything. There is no news worse than that.

When Jesus died on that wooden cross for us, we were given our only opportunity for victory over our sin and its consequence of death. That's not just *news*. . .that's the *best* news you've ever heard.

6

The Church

Do I really have to go?

When we were kids, my little brother and I had the same "spirited discussion" with our parents every Sunday morning.

"Wake up, boys. It's time for church," my mom would say in a sweet and gentle voice. But since video-game-palooza kept us up too late the night before, and because we hated church, we would grunt something unintelligible—but argumentative—in response. That grunt on our part always marked the end of the sweet and gentle on Mom's part.

"I said 'Get up!'" she would bark. "We've only got an hour before church starts!" As I tossed the covers aside in protest, I decried her abuse of parental authority. With emphatic lamentations, I bemoaned the fact that church was boring, or that I got nothing out of it, or that the people were judgmental and mean, or some other reality about the church that was harsh (but true).

Not only did the pastor preach from the King James Version of the Bible—in all its archaic glory—but he also used lots of seventeen-syllable theological terms to go along with the pointless ramblings he called sermons. *(Though I can't prove it, I believe ADD and ADHD somehow stem from attending this kind of church as a kid.)*

But it wasn't just the church's language that made the weekly experience completely irrelevant to my life. The average age of the congregation was just shy of infinity. . .old people everywhere. And by most measures, they had zero desire to reach our community with the message of the Gospel. They were too busy with a fish fry here and a potluck there.

It was for these reasons—and many others—that I asked my weekly question: "Do I really have to go to church?"

I hated every second of church. I considered it to be a torturous way to kill multiple hours from my precious weekend. It was just an awful place to be.

As I write this, I'm very pleased to say that this same church is now a place of love and grace. As a result, it is growing and deeply affecting the lives of families in its community. The church has come a long way. But when I was a kid, it was a bad church, and nobody wants to go to a bad church. Heck, nobody even wants to go to a bad *movie* or a bad *restaurant*. But just because one restaurant is dirty doesn't mean they all are. Just because one movie stinks doesn't mean they all will. Likewise, just because one church is bad doesn't mean they all are.

I won't try to sugarcoat it; as a whole, the church in North

America is losing its voice in today's culture. According to some of the latest research available, a mere 20 percent of Americans can be found in church on Sunday mornings.[4] The church has been labeled as boring, irrelevant, and judgmental on more than one occasion; but the unnecessary damage it has suffered from frequent stories of financial scandals and sexual misconduct has been far more detrimental. As a result, the church has made it easy for society to simply hit the mute button.

But it hasn't always been that way. . .

Old-School Church

There was a time when culture paid close attention to the church. In fact, it wouldn't be an overstatement to say there was a time when society was even *shaped* by the church. But, sadly, that time was long ago.

The early history of Christianity is recorded in the book of Acts, which tells about the birth of the church on the Day of Pentecost when the Holy Spirit filled Jesus' disciples, how it grew so rapidly, and its success in spreading the message of Jesus Christ to the rest of the world. The first church—or the early church, as some scholars call it—was so effective because it was made up of people who were committed to living like Jesus lived.

A lot of Jesus' public life was spent preaching. In the first chapter of Mark's Gospel, Jesus says that was the reason He came.

*Very early in the morning, while it was still
dark, Jesus got up, left the house and went off to
a solitary place, where he prayed. Simon and his
companions went to look for him, and when they
found him, they exclaimed: "Everyone is looking
for you!" Jesus replied, "Let us go somewhere else—
to the nearby villages—so I can preach there also.
That is why I have come." (Mark 1:35–38)*

The members of the very first church were just as serious about preaching. On the Day of Pentecost, Peter stood up and delivered a message in downtown Jerusalem that compelled *three thousand* people to begin following Jesus. You can read that "in-your-face" sermon in Acts 2:14–41 (or one by Stephen in Acts 7:1–53, or another one by Paul in Acts 22:1–21).

But there was more to Jesus than just words, of course. He performed unexplainable miracles (which we talked about in chapter 3). Again, the first church followed His example. In Acts 3:1-10, Peter and John meet a crippled man who had been born without the use of his legs. In the name of Jesus, they changed that:

*Peter said, "Silver or gold I do not have, but what
I do have I give you. In the name of Jesus Christ of
Nazareth, walk." Taking him by the right hand,
he helped him up, and instantly the man's feet and
ankles became strong. He jumped to his feet and
began to walk. Then he went with them into the*

temple courts, walking and jumping, and praising
God. (Acts 3:6–8)

In case you were wondering whether this was a fluke or a one-hit-wonder by Jesus' followers, now known as the apostles, check out what the writer of Acts says just two chapters later:

The apostles performed many miraculous signs and
wonders among the people. And all the believers
used to meet together in Solomon's Colonnade. No
one else dared join them, even though they were
highly regarded by the people. Nevertheless, more
and more men and women believed in the Lord
and were added to their number. As a result, people
brought the sick into the streets and laid them
on beds and mats so that at least Peter's shadow
might fall on some of them as he passed by. Crowds
gathered also from the towns around Jerusalem,
bringing their sick and those tormented by impure
spirits, and all of them were healed. (Acts 5:12–16)

Jesus healed people, so His disciples healed people. It's as simple as that. Of course, most will agree that the only action that trumps healing a sick person is resurrecting a dead person. We know from the Gospels that Jesus raised at least three people from the dead during His earthly ministry: Jairus's daughter (Mark 5), the son of a widow in the town of Nain (Luke 7), and Lazarus (John 11).

Once again, we see the early followers of Jesus performing the same miraculous deed. For example, the apostle Paul raised a dead guy during a lengthy church service one night:

> On the first day of the week we came together to break bread. Paul spoke to the people and, because he intended to leave the next day, kept on talking until midnight. There were many lamps in the upstairs room where we were meeting. Seated in a window was a young man named Eutychus, who was sinking into a deep sleep as Paul talked on and on. When he was sound asleep, he fell to the ground from the third story and was picked up dead. Paul went down, threw himself on the young man and put his arms around him. "Don't be alarmed," he said. "He's alive!" Then he went upstairs again and broke bread and ate. After talking until daylight, he left. The people took the young man home alive and were greatly comforted. (Acts 20:7–12)

Growing the congregation by thousands in just one day? Healing the sick? Raising the dead? Does that sound like any church you know? By the way, we shouldn't forget that the early church accomplished all of this while being hunted and persecuted by religious and governmental leaders.

That's just old-school church at its finest.

So, what happened? Why are the churches of today so different from the very first church? Where's the growth? The influence and excitement? *The miracles?* Is it even possible for today's churches to have that kind of power and effectiveness?

Absolutely! That is, if you and I are willing to *be* the church in the same way the first disciples were the church.

The Church That Jesus Built

Two thousand years ago, Jesus took His disciples on a lengthy trek to a place called Caesarea Philippi to have an important conversation with them. Named after an emperor of Rome (and simultaneously a Jewish king), Caesarea Philippi would have surely been a splendid place. Located in the lush and fertile foothills of Mount Hermon, the city enjoyed a high vantage point, perched atop a massive rock formation at an elevation of 1,150 feet.

But for all of the city's majesty, the residents of ancient Caesarea Philippi were probably just as confused about "religious stuff" as many of us are. That's because the city was little more than a collection of temples. There were temples built to honor Roman emperors. There were temples built to honor Greek gods. And even a few Syrian gods had temples dedicated to them in the city. There were almost as many temples in Caesarea Philippi as there are hot dog stands in New York City. But it was in this highly religious setting that Jesus had one of His most important conversations with the twelve disciples. Here's how Matthew recounts it:

> *When Jesus came to the region of Caesarea*
> *Philippi, he asked his disciples, "Who do people*

say the Son of Man is?" They replied, "Some say John the Baptist; others say Elijah; and still others, Jeremiah or one of the prophets."

But what about you?" he asked. "Who do you say I am?"

Simon Peter answered, "You are the Messiah, the Son of the living God."

Jesus replied, "Blessed are you, Simon son of Jonah, for this was not revealed to you by flesh and blood, but by my Father in heaven. And I tell you that you are Peter, and on this rock I will build my church, and the gates of Hades will not overcome it. I will give you the keys of the kingdom of heaven; whatever you bind on earth will be bound in heaven, and whatever you loose on earth will be loosed in heaven." Then he ordered his disciples not to tell anyone that he was the Messiah. (Matthew 16:13–20)

On the surface, this short story might make you think that Jesus was narcissistic or suffering from low self-esteem or worrying about people's opinions of Him. Not true; God doesn't lose sleep over what humans think of Him. The real reason Jesus took His disciples on this long field trip was to discuss His true identity.

Jesus began by asking a simple question: *"Hey guys, what are you hearing from the crowds? What are they saying on Twitter? Who do they think I am?"* It isn't surprising that Jesus received several different answers to His question. Just like today, crowds tend to have varying opinions of high-profile leaders. But then Jesus asked a more pointed question. He wanted to know who *the disciples* thought He was. *"All right fellas, what about you? Who do you really think I am?"*

Peter responded to Jesus and said, *"You are the Messiah, the Son of the living God."* In other words, Peter said, "Jesus, You're who we've been waiting for. Without a doubt, You're the anointed one, God's Son."

Um. . .that's a big deal. In case you missed it, Peter called Jesus *God.* When Peter replied this way, Jesus declared that the humble fisherman would be a blessed man because God the Father had revealed this eternity-changing truth to him.

Then Jesus began talking about this thing called church.

It's no accident that Jesus focused discussion on Himself *before* turning the topic of the conversation to the church. That's because if we really want to *understand church*, we must first *recognize Jesus.* If we don't know *who* Jesus is, we will never know *what* the church is. That's because, without Jesus, there is no church. Literally. He said so Himself.

Jesus said He would personally build the church. After Peter declared that Jesus was the Christ—that is, God Himself—Jesus chose His words carefully and said, *"I tell you that you are Peter, and on this rock I will build my church."* You might not know this, but Jesus changed Peter's name early in their relationship (see John 1:42). Peter's given name was Simon, but Jesus dubbed him Peter, which translates into English as "rock." And don't forget, they were standing in view of the massive rock formation that served as the solid base of Caesarea Philippi.

When it came to building the church, Jesus wasn't going to appoint a religious leader to head up the project. He wasn't even willing to entrust an angel with the task. If the church was going to accomplish what Jesus expected of it, it would have to be built perfectly, so Jesus shouldered the responsibility Himself.

Equally important, Jesus said that His church would be *unstoppable*. After claiming He would be the brains and brawn behind His church, Jesus made a statement about His future work: *"I will build my church, and the gates of Hades will not overcome it."* Just so you know, *Hades* is the Greek word for hell. Jesus said that hell itself would not be able to stop His church. *(I'm not absolutely certain, but this statement might be the very first instance of smack talk in history.)*

In this one sentence, Jesus basically says, "It's on! My church will thunder across the planet with the message of My salvation, and nothing, not even the gates of hell, will be able to stop it!" It was a bold statement—especially because weak and sinful humans were to play such an important role in its construction. But Jesus nonetheless made the declaration. Other inventors and designers have made similar claims on behalf of their creations in the past. For example, in the early 1900s, the builders of the *Titanic* had the audacity to declare their ship unsinkable.

Hmm. . .we know how that turned out.

But after roughly two thousand years, the bold claim Jesus made about His church is still accurate. The church is still undefeated, still the heavyweight champion of the world. It's not because the church hasn't had its enemies; it had dangerous enemies the very moment it was birthed. It's simply that none of those enemies have ever been able to stop the church.

Plenty have tried, of course. Yemelian Yaroslavsky was one of them.

Yaroslavsky was a Russian politician, journalist, and revolutionary who lived through World War I and most of World War II. However, he was best known as an outspoken atheist who served as the chairman of Joseph Stalin's ruthless League of the Militant Godless.

Yeah, that was really the group's name.

As one of the leaders in Stalin's cruel anti-religious campaign, Yaroslavsky closed churches, shut down theological schools, and exiled pastors to ghastly labor camps. . .that is, if he didn't kill them. But in spite of his efforts to crush the church, the Russian atheist eventually confessed, "Christianity is like a nail. The harder you strike it the deeper it goes."

Yaroslavsky wasted his life trying to defeat the church that Christ had built, only to find that it was unconquerable. . .just as Jesus had said. To this very day, the church that Jesus built is alive and well in all corners of the globe. . .even in places where it is violently persecuted and oppressed.

It's a good thing the church is unconquerable; it has a huge mission to accomplish.

Mission: Imparted

In simple terms, the church is supposed to change the world. That's the task Jesus imparted to us. Just change the world. *No problem, right?* Since no other agency or organization has ever accomplished that task, the church definitely has its work cut out for it. Fortunately, the church isn't an inanimate building; that's merely a sanctuary. The church itself is a group of *people* who are committed to living how Jesus said to live.

So, how did Jesus say we should live? Well, here are just a *few* of the practices Jesus said should be a part of our life as His people, the church:

- Helping others (Matthew 25:33–40)
- Making disciples (Matthew 28:19–20)
- Preaching (Mark 16:15)
- Worshipping (Romans 12:1)
- Giving (2 Corinthians 8:7)
- Encouraging one another (1 Thessalonians 5:11)
- Praying (1 Timothy 2:8)
- Studying God's words (1 Timothy 4:13)
- Teaching (2 Timothy 2:2)
- Caring for the helpless (James 1:27)
- Healing (James 5:14–16)
- Loving one another (1 John 3:11)

This is only a partial list; there are easily a couple dozen more ways to operate as the church of Jesus Christ. Perhaps the most straightforward description of what the church should do is found in Acts 2:42:

> *They devoted themselves to the apostles' teaching and to fellowship, to the breaking of bread and to prayer.*

That one verse contains four essential aspects of the church. For starters, the first disciples were focused on understanding truth in all its purity (devoted to the apostles' teaching). But they also wanted to provide a place of belonging (the fellowship) for those who were coming into the faith. To move forward, they were always looking backward to the sacrifice of Jesus on the cross, symbolized by the Lord's Supper (the breaking of bread). Finally, they kept in constant contact with God (prayer) because they knew where their power came from.

We take this verse so seriously at our church that every afternoon at 2:42 p.m., members of our faith community pause to pray through the habits found in Acts 2:42. We simply set an alarm on our smartphones for 2:42 p.m., and then we ask God to unify us through (1) the apostles' teaching, (2) fellowship, (3) breaking of bread, and (4) prayer. Ever since we started doing that, our church has grown numerically, spiritually, and relationally.

Feel free to join us in prayer tomorrow afternoon. . .and then in church on Sunday.

Church Search

Okay, unless you live in Central Florida, you probably can't come to our church. But that doesn't mean you can't be a part of a strong and healthy congregation where you live. Unfortunately, finding a good church is easier said than done. When searching for the right church, you'll need to look beyond the comfortable chairs, free coffee, and great-sounding band.

After all, some churches have stained-glass windows. . . *others have stained hearts.*

Though no *perfect* church exists, healthy churches can be readily identified by traits they have in common. Though there are several traits we could mention, let's explore three of the most important ones.

1. Healthy churches genuinely love one another.

On a Sunday night—January 30, 2011, to be exact—police officers in Fletcher, North Carolina, responded to their dispatcher's report of a huge fight. But these law enforcement agents weren't called to a school, a sporting event, or even a local bar.

Nope. They were called out to a Baptist church.

Almost thirty police officers—*from five different agencies*—were part of the crowd control at Greater New Zion Baptist Church that evening. Heated words and hot heads had catapulted some members past arguing to outright fighting. In the aftermath of the skirmish, many of the church members were embarrassed over their words and actions. The pastor later said his church's behavior, "is not the way for Christians to be Christians."

That's the understatement of the year.

How will this church be recognized and remembered in its community? As the church with the great preaching? As the church that fed the homeless? As the church that helped struggling families? Even if the church does all those things and more, it will probably be remembered as the church that fought itself.

That church's actions stand in stark contrast to the command Jesus gave His followers. We've already mentioned it before, but it bears repeating because it's the way Jesus said we'd be recognized as His disciples:

> *"A new command I give you: Love one another. As I have loved you, so you must love one another. By this everyone will know that you are my disciples, if you love one another." (John 13:34–35)*

If you are looking for a great church, look for one where the people genuinely love one another. I didn't say, "Look for a church that *says* it loves one another." I said, "Look for a church that *genuinely* loves one another." Here are some questions to help you gauge how well the church does that:

1. Do they handle disagreements (or conflict) with grace and respect. . .or with pouting and shouting?

2. When someone is caught in sin, does the church respond with sincere and total forgiveness or with resentment and condemnation?

3. When a person experiences a blessing, does the church celebrate with him or her? Likewise, when someone faces an upset or loss, does the church rally around and grieve with that person?

4. How well are different groups integrated? For example, are teenagers and senior citizens encouraged to mingle and given opportunities to do so? Or are the various groups isolated from one another?

5. How close is the church to Paul's description of love in 1 Corinthians 13:1–8?

A church's love is the beginning point of all that follows. If church members cannot love one another, they probably won't get much else right, either. But loving one another is just the first requirement for a strong, healthy church. Let's look at two more.

2. Healthy churches preach God's words unapologetically.

I'm going to put this as nicely as I can: *some churches have turned into sissies.*

You can always spot a "sissy church" by what it preaches . . .and by what it *doesn't* preach. Some churches have allowed philosophy and people's preferences to determine their preaching instead of the Bible. For example, some churches no longer preach that Jesus is the *only* source of salvation. After all, to say that Jesus is the only way to have eternal life is considered intolerant and narrow-minded these days. Not that these churches care, but Jesus disagrees with them point blank:

> Jesus answered, "I am the way and the truth and the life. No one comes to the Father except through me." (John 14:6)

Jesus didn't say He was *a* way to the Father; He said He was *the* way, as in, the *only* way. This error about Jesus is doctrinal in nature and absolutely inexcusable, but it's not the only error sissy churches make when it comes to preaching.

Other "sissy churches" allow culture and popular opinion to dictate what they believe and preach. For example, a growing number of churches no longer preach that homosexuality is a sinful lifestyle, even though it's denounced every single time it's mentioned in Scripture. (I could easily have picked a different controversial subject—for instance, divorce or abortion—but let's face it, homosexuality is at the forefront of our society's attention these days.) To hear churches and their leaders proclaim anything other than a biblical message on this issue is sad. . .and simultaneously comical.

Those poor pastors have to twist Scripture really hard to turn "Do not!" into "It's okay."

That said, pastors shouldn't beat down homosexuals (or alcoholics or gossipers) with condemning messages; but neither should they alter what God's words mean. When you go to the doctor, you need the truth. . .no matter how bad it might be. When you go to the mechanic, you need the truth. . .no matter how expensive it might be. When you go to church, you need the truth. . .no matter how much it means you must change.

For the most part, sissy preaching is the fault of church leaders—primarily, the pastors—but it can trickle down to everyone in the church. As you are learning about a church, ask reflective questions on the messages being proclaimed:

1. Does the church's preaching match God's words? In other words, does the preaching say what the Bible says?

2. Does the church preach the *entire* Bible? It's easy to use the same familiar passages again and again, but that neglects so much of what God is trying to communicate to us. A pastor doesn't have to preach through all sixty-six books in one sermon every Sunday, but there's also more to the Bible than just John 3:16.

3. Does the church's preaching bring about transformation in people's lives? The purpose of preaching isn't to fill up thirty minutes of time during the worship service. The purpose of preaching is to change lives. If your life isn't being changed, it's because you're not applying what you hear. . .or you're not hearing God's words to begin with. Which is it?

You need all of the truth all of the time, so make sure the preaching you're listening to is providing it. Don't be afraid to ask difficult questions about preaching. That's the only way to know if the church is doing what God expects of us. Speaking of God's expectations. . .

3. Healthy churches intentionally reach the lost.

In my early twenties, I visited an esteemed and historical

church in a major city in the South. The church's colossal building had a huge steeple and stained-glass windows everywhere. . . .even in the bathrooms. They had also saved some of the wooden pews from the original church building, which dated back to the early nineteenth century.

I arrived early enough to meet the pastor and a few other leaders in the church. Being a youth pastor at the time, I asked them about their youth ministry program, hoping I could attend their morning gathering before returning for the main service.

"We don't have a youth ministry, really," said one older woman. And that's when I noticed that the entire group of people I was talking to were old—like *in-their-nineties* old! There wasn't a single person below the age of forty—*let alone my age*—to be found.

After suffering through a Sunday school class for "young families" that didn't have any young families in it, I was en route to the main service when I bumped into an elderly lady I had met earlier. She and I walked to the sanctuary together, and while we waited for the service to begin, I talked with a few of her friends about the beauty of the sanctuary, the old wooden pews, the stained-glass windows, and all the other items of décor found inside the sanctuary.

Looking around, I posed this question: "What is it that your church is known for in the community?"

No one answered my question. They seemed perplexed by it, actually. I asked again, "What is it that your church does in the community that gives you the reputation of being a church?"

Crickets.

Thinking I still wasn't being clear, I simply said, "When people think of your church, they think, *Oh, that's the church that...*"

And that's when it clicked with one of the petite ladies standing across from me. "Oh, I see," she said. "I tell you what our church is known for. When General Sherman was marching through the South during the Civil War, burning town after town, we rang our church bell to warn people he was coming."

I smiled as cordially as I could. I wanted to say, "That's your claim to fame? One hundred and fifty years ago...you rang a bell? What about *since* the time when slavery was abolished?"

The church's mission is simple to articulate: *we're supposed to turn atheists into missionaries.* Our God-given job is to lead people to Christ and to help them lead others to Christ. No matter what a church accomplishes—or how beautiful their sanctuary is—if they don't reach the lost with the love of Jesus, they've missed out on what's most important. Here are some questions to help you gauge how well the church is accomplishing its mission:

1. Is the church outwardly focused, or are they simply existing for themselves? Are their programs and ministries geared for people who are *outside* the church or are they restricted to people who are already *in* the church?

2. What portion of the total budget is given to missions, evangelism, and/or outreach? Do they spend all their money on themselves, or are they actively trying to reach a lost world with the Good News of Jesus Christ?

3. Does the church actually *go* into the surrounding community (like Jesus said we should in Matthew 28:19–20), or do they just *invite* the community to come to them?

4. How much does the church look like the community it's in? Do the people inside the church look like the people walking past it outside?

This isn't an exhaustive list, of course, but loving one another, preaching God's words, and reaching the lost are three of the most important characteristics of a healthy church, for sure. When searching for a church, you should factor in as much information as possible. And don't neglect to pray about this important decision. You're not the only one who wants you to be an integral part of a great church. God does, too.

So, Do I Have to Go to Church?

I've been a pastor for more than half my life, which means I've heard it all.

"I don't go to church because the church is filled with hypocrites."

Yes, there are a number of hypocrites at every church. Those people put on a mask and go to church hoping that no one will ever find out their real identity. It's sad, but it's true. However, that's an awful reason not to go to church. After all, if you avoid *every* place that's filled with hypocrites, you'd never go to Walmart or Applebee's or the movie theater, either. Hypocrites are everywhere. Get over it and get to church.

"I don't have to go to church to be a Christian." It's true; you don't have to go to church to be a Christian. You don't have to go to Fenway Park to be a Red Sox fan, either. But if you want to be an *obedient* Christian, you need to go to church (see Hebrews 10:24–25).

I could make an extensive list of the reasons I've heard for skipping church:

- *"I don't have to go to church to go to heaven."* (Umm… going to church doesn't get you to heaven in the first place.)

- *"I had my feelings hurt at church."* (Is that the only place you've ever had your feelings hurt?)

- *"I don't care for organized religion."* (Most churches aren't organized *enough*!)

I could go on and on, but I won't. I truly believe that when a person understands who Jesus is and discovers the right church, they move from a mind-set of *having* to go to church to *getting* to go to church. Church should never be looked at as an obligation, but an opportunity. God has invited you to partner with Him as He works in this world.

Church isn't something we *do*; it is something we have the chance to *be*.

If you don't have a great church home, I sincerely hope you find a strong one that allows you to grow in Christ and share Him with the world. If you do have a great church, then I hope you'll honor the commitments you've made to your spiritual family through investment and service.

Session 6

The Church

Do I really have to go?

Big Idea: Even though we might not always understand the church, God designed it perfectly. If we conform to His design, we'll be a blessing to others.

Passage: 1 Corinthians 12:12–27

Discussion Starter: *The Human Body: A Pop Quiz*

1. Who has more bones, a healthy baby or a healthy adult?

You might guess that they have the same number of bones, since a baby is nothing more than a very tiny adult. But if there *were* a difference between the two, you'd probably guess that an adult has more bones than a baby, simply because the adult is bigger and has had much more time to develop. You'd be wrong on both counts. The reality is, a healthy baby has more bones than a healthy adult. *A lot more, in fact.*

A healthy baby is born with 270–300 bones in his or her body (depending on who's counting); a healthy adult has 206. God designed babies' skeletons this way so they can compress in certain areas and squeeze through the birth canal without getting broken. But as the baby grows, certain bones—such as those in the skull and spine—begin to fuse together, leaving an adult with the perfect number of bones: 206.

2. Which of your hands is bigger, your left or your right?

Why wouldn't they both be the same? After all, both hands have five fingers. . .and you've been growing both of them the exact same length of time!

But the truth is, one of the two is slightly bigger than the other; determining which one it is depends on which hand is your dominant hand. Your dominant hand is typically the bigger of the two because its muscles get used more often—throwing a ball, opening a can, or writing a note—causing it to be a wee bit larger and stronger.

3. Which of your lungs is bigger, your left or your right?

Unlike your hands, it has nothing to do with which lung you use the most, mainly because you use both lungs with every single breath.

Everybody's right lung is just a little bit bigger than their left lung, because the left lung has to share space with the heart, which is located in the center of your chest but turned slightly to the left.

4. What is the purpose of eyebrows?

It's essentially hair that's growing on your forehead—not on your *head*, but your *forehead*. It sounds strange to consider, but if you've ever burnt off your eyebrows lighting the grill, you're the one who *looks* strange.

Eyebrows actually serve several unique purposes. Because they are arched over our eyes like an umbrella, they do a great job of funneling water and sweat away from our eyes. They also capture debris and keep it from entering our eyes. Eyebrows even provide a little shade from the bright sunlight.

At all costs, protect those eyebrows!

5. How many cells die in your body every second?

I'll give you a hint: *a lot.*

On average, 3 million cells die in your body every single second of the day. That translates to 180 million cells per minute. . .which is more than 10 billion per hour! In a typical day, your body suffers the loss of roughly 240 billion cells!

But don't be alarmed; you can afford to lose that many cells because you're made up of about 35 trillion of them. . .and a trillion is a whole bunch.

So how did you do on the quiz?

Don't get upset if you didn't do so well; the intricacies of our design perplex even the most intelligent scientists. After studying our anatomy, most people are left with a sense of awe at just how wonderful our bodies are.

The way God designed us is, in a word, *perfect*. For example, our retinas alone are made up of more than 100 million rods and cones to help us see, and our eyes produce tears to keep our fragile visual organs clean. Equally impressive is the fact that our stomach lining replaces itself every three or four days so that the acids in our stomachs that digest our food don't digest *us*. There's a reason God made us the way He did. Everything has a place and a purpose. As we study our bodies, we begin to discover that there's a reason behind God's design.

The same is true of the church. Even though we might not always understand the church, God designed it perfectly, as well. If the church operates according to God's design, it will be a blessing to others.

Opening Questions

1. Which aspect(s) of our bodies do you find most interesting? Why?

2. Scientists, doctors, and other experts are far from understanding exactly how our bodies work the way they do. Is that because God's design is flawed or because there are flaws in our understanding of His design? Both? Neither? Something else entirely?

3. What does God's design of our bodies say about God Himself?

4. In the New Testament, the Bible often calls the church a "body" or the "body of Christ." Why do you think God's

words describe the church as a body?

5. Do you think God designed the church with the same attention to detail evident in the design of our bodies? Why or why not?

6. What happens when a human body doesn't function properly (through disease, drug use, lack of exercise, etc.)? What happens when a church doesn't function properly?

Bible Passage
1 Corinthians 12:12–27

Just as a body, though one, has many parts, but all its many parts form one body, so it is with Christ. For we were all baptized by one Spirit so as to form one body—whether Jews or Greeks, slave or free—and we were all given the one Spirit to drink. Now the body is not made up of one part but of many.

Now if the foot should say, "Because I am not a hand, I do not belong to the body," it would not for that reason stop being part of the body. And if the ear should say, "Because I am not an eye, I do not belong to the body," it would not for that reason stop being part of the body. If the whole body were an eye, where would the sense of hearing be? If the whole body were an ear, where would the sense of smell be? But in fact God has placed the parts in the body, every one of them, just as he wanted them to be. If they were all one part, where would the body be? As it is, there are many parts, but one body.

The eye cannot say to the hand, "I don't need you!" And the head cannot say to the feet, "I don't need you!" On the contrary, those parts of the body that seem to be weaker are indispensable, and the parts that we think are less honorable we treat with special honor. And the parts that are unpresentable are treated with special modesty, while our presentable parts need no special treatment. But God has put the body together, giving greater honor to the parts that lacked it, so that there should be no division in the body, but that its parts should have equal concern for each other. If one part suffers, every part suffers with it; if one part is honored, every part rejoices with it.

Now you are the body of Christ, and each one of you is a part of it.

Study Questions

1. Twice in his letter to the Corinthians the apostle Paul said that God designed the church just as He wanted it. In verse 18, he wrote, *"God has placed the parts in the body. . .just as he wanted them to be"*; and in verse 24, he asserted, *"God has put the body together."* Why is that particular detail significant enough to repeat?

2. What would Paul say to someone in the church who thinks they're more important than someone else? Likewise, what would he say to someone who thinks they are less important?

3. Can you name some of the "parts" in your church, and who fills them?

4. Why did Paul say the body of Christ needs its various parts? What happens if it's missing a part (or two)?

Deeper Questions

1. How well does your church comply with 1 Corinthians 12:12–27? How could it improve?

2. Though the church has existed for two thousand years, there has been ample confusion during that time about what the church is and what it does. Some have thought it was filled with "atheists" (http://itslikethis.org/?p=775), and others thought it was filled with "incestuous cannibals" (http://itslikethis.org/?p=771). Who is to blame for the misconceptions: the church or the world? Why?

3. When a church functions as a healthy body, how does it benefit its members? How does it benefit the lost?

Application Questions

1. What part of the body are you? How do you know?

2. Do you genuinely suffer when another part of the body of Christ suffers? Do you genuinely rejoice when another part of the body of Christ is honored? Why or why not?

3. In what way(s) can you make the body of Christ stronger or more complete?

Final Word

There's no doubt about it; today's church faces a harsh reality when it looks in the mirror. Too many churches have abysmal—but nonetheless deserved—reputations, and are rightly criticized for their failures. It's not hard to find people who don't trust the church or people who don't like the church or people who are just confused by the church.

- *"Why is the church so divided? It has thousands of different denominations. Why can't they all just get along?"*

- *"The church ranges from hypocritical to outright scandalous."*

- *"I don't understand why church has to be so boring."*

- *"I thought the church was supposed to love people, but there are whole groups in our culture that the church seems to hate."*

- *"I tried church a few times; it didn't do any good. Pretty useless if you ask me."*

Yes, the church has gotten some things wrong across the years, but when it operates as God intended, it offers something everyone needs that they cannot get anywhere else: the life-changing love of Jesus Christ. That's the church's specialty!

But for the church to accomplish its mission, we must operate as God intended and as God designed. Based on 1 Corinthians 12, it's crystal clear how God wants the church to live and operate: *as one.* Paul said that we are *"all baptized by one Spirit into one body."* There is only *one* Spirit, and He put us together in *one* particular body. No matter our background, our former identities, or our shortcomings and failures, together we comprise *one* body . . .*the* body of Christ.

The best sports teams understand the concept of *one,* and that's why they win more often than the other teams. For example, the champions of any given Super Bowl could very well have players on it from all walks of life—*different upbringings, different experiences, different philosophies, and different talents*—but when they take the field, they take it as *one* team. The team that plays "as one" is usually the team that wins.

The church must also operate as one. It must be united in love and focused on a singular, God-given mission. The church is a special group of people on a special mission to change the world. Church was never intended to be a "place to go." If that's the way you're currently looking at the church, there's something wrong.

In spite of its setbacks and its faltering reputation, the church is still the group of people God is using to change the world. Even better, He wants *you* to be a major part of it. In fact, if you're committed to following Jesus but aren't plugged into a life-giving church, then somewhere there's a church that's missing one of its parts. Go find your fit.

7

Heaven and Hell

What happens when I die?

I'm from Florida. I've lived here my entire life, and I'm accustomed to the three different kinds of weather the Sunshine State has to offer: *heat, humidity,* and *hurricanes.* We honestly don't know which of these is worst.

But since I speak at a lot of conferences and churches every year, I do a lot of traveling. I pack pretty light for the most part: a few changes of clothes, my laptop, and my Bible. But that only works for places like Georgia, Texas, or Oklahoma in July. *All bets are off when it comes to Minnesota in January.*

For Floridians, that kind of trip can be fatal; it's been medically proven that our blood ceases to flow at 48 degrees Fahrenheit.

Watching me pack for a midwinter speaking engagement in Minnesota is a spectacle to behold. For starters, it's a two-day endeavor just to find a store in Florida that even sells apparel capable of combating what Minnesotans call a "breeze" (the howling, eyeball-freezing, cyclonic gusts of death) or temps that are "chilly" (the polar-bear-frightening, hypothermia-inducing, Siberian climate). I actually remember asking a salesman in a department store for gloves before one trip. Mind you, we were both wearing the official footwear of Florida: flip-flops. He replied, "Why do you need those? You live in Florida."

When I told him I was going to Minnesota, he winced.

Then there's the whole packing side of things. It's no longer a "single carry-on suitcase" kind of trip. No, when I have to travel north of the Mason-Dixon Line in the winter, I actually hire a team of Sherpas to help me lug all my survival gear. (Side note for my fellow Floridians: the TSA at Tampa International Airport really frowns on your packing firewood, gasoline, and a butane torch.) Yep, it takes a lot for Floridians to venture very far north in the winter.

And that's for a three-day trip. . .to somewhere else on earth.

Now, just imagine if you were preparing for a trip—off this rock called Earth—that will last for all of eternity. To be clear, that's a one-way trip that's gonna last a *really* long time.

How would you prepare? What sort of decisions would you make prior to leaving?

On the Fly

I find it immensely strange that every human knows this trip is ahead of them, but so few make intentional preparations for it. When we travel, most of us consult multiple websites to ensure the best deal on airfare, flip over to the Weather Channel to get an update on the forecast, and even Google a few fun things to do at our chosen destination. We give more thought to a weeklong vacation in Cancun than we do to our eternal destination. Talk about making plans *on the fly*. . . .

Even Benjamin Franklin, a really, really smart guy, did this. Just after his eighty-fourth birthday in January 1790, the world-famous American inventor received a letter from his friend, the Reverend Ezra Stiles, president of Yale, inquiring about the statesman's beliefs. It was humbly and affectionately received by Franklin, and he penned his ministerial friend a well-considered response:

> *You desire to know something of my religion. It is the first time I have been questioned upon it. But I cannot take your curiosity amiss, and shall endeavor in a few words to gratify it. Here is my creed: As to Jesus of Nazareth, my opinion of whom you particularly desire, I think his system of morals and his religion, as he left them to us, the best the world ever saw or is likely to see; but I apprehend it has received various corrupting changes, and I have, with most of the present dissenters in England, some doubts as to his divinity; though it is a question I do not dogmatize upon, having never studied it, and think it needless to busy myself with it now, when I expect soon an opportunity of knowing the truth with less trouble.*[5]

In other words, Franklin basically said, "That's a great question, and I fully understand that my answer to it affects all of my eternity. But I haven't given it much thought. . .and I'm too old to start now." Just a few weeks after sending his reply, Franklin took the unavoidable trip that every human faces. He finally had his "opportunity of knowing the truth."

We can only hope it was with as little "trouble" as possible.

Benjamin Franklin isn't the only one confused about the hereafter but unmotivated to discover the truth. In late 2013, the Barna Group released the findings of some research they'd conducted on Americans' beliefs concerning heaven, hell, and the afterlife in general. According to the survey, 81 percent of Americans believe there's an afterlife of some sort. In other words, the vast majority think there's something that happens "next."

A slightly smaller percentage, 76 percent, believe that heaven exists (though their descriptions of heaven varied), and 71 percent believe hell exists (though, again, there were some major contrasts about what it will be like). It's certainly not a huge difference, but the 5 percent gap between belief in heaven and belief in hell is revealing. Why wouldn't the number of people who believe in heaven be the exact same as the number of people who believe in hell?

Here's where it gets even more interesting. A whopping 64 percent of Americans believe they'll go to heaven (though their reasons for believing so are very different across the survey sample), and only 0.5 percent (that's one-half of 1 percent) expect to wind up in hell.[6] I'd say those numbers are spot on. In fact, I've met only one person in my pastoral career who thought he was going to hell. When I asked him where he thought he'd spend eternity, he replied, "I'm gonna bust the gates of hell wide open."

Well, at least he wasn't going to be surprised. . . .

Nobody's willing to actually *say* it, but survey after survey shows that millions of people believe that heaven is simply our default setting for eternity (even though we've already learned that the default setting of our nature is sinful and deserving of death and separation from God). In other words, people believe they'll go to heaven, because. . .well. . .they just can't see themselves going to hell.

Umm. . .that's not how it works.

Perhaps the most honest group in the Barna study was the 24 percent who said they have "no idea" what will happen to them when they die. Okay, fair enough, but what are they doing to find out? Are they content to wing it, even though it's such an important matter? Are they just going to rip a page from Ben Franklin's playbook and find out when they get there, wherever "there" may be?

"What happens when I die?" is a really great question. It deserves a great answer.

Up? Down? Sideways? Around Again?

Fortunately, the Bible includes crystal clear teaching to help us answer that question the right way. God's words don't leave anything to chance on this matter. They spell out the truth concerning what happens when we die. . .starting with the number of alternatives that exist. According to God's words, there are just two: heaven or hell. Granted, you may have heard of other options, ranging from *religious* to *ridiculous*, but the truth is, every living soul will spend eternity in either heaven *or* hell.

That means purgatory, the temporary place of suffering for people who need to be a *little more purified* before entering heaven, is one of the "religious" options that needs to be put on the chopping block. Even though a lot of religious people talk about it, there are several problems with the concept of purgatory, beginning with the fact that the word isn't found in the Bible. (Okay, the word *Trinity* isn't found in the Bible either, but we believe it's legitimate because of reasons already discussed.) More damaging to the credibility of purgatory is the destructive impact it would have on the salvation Jesus offers if it did exist. If purgatory were real, it would imply that Jesus' death on the cross wasn't *quite* sufficient to forgive us of our sin. It'd be like God saying, "Yeah, Jesus suffered on the cross to forgive your sins. . .but you need to suffer some, too." Remember what we learned in chapter 5: either we are rescued by Jesus Christ alone. . .or we aren't rescued at all.

Another religious-sounding option that must be dismissed is reincarnation—the idea that people, after they die, come back to a different life and a different body so they can merge with God and experience ultimate reality by living the next life better than the last. Apparently, reincarnation can happen as many times as necessary, but each life greatly influences the next. . .*for good or bad.*

Don't worry about all the ways this contradicts God's words; just take a moment to reflect on the number of serious flaws inherent in the system itself. For example, who gets to decide what a person comes back as? In other words, who's in charge of deciding the fate of another person's soul? Further, what are the guidelines for success and failure? How much good must we do to ensure that we don't come back as plankton in the next life? Finally, if we struggled with our sinful nature in our past life, and the life before that, and the life before that, what makes us think we won't struggle with it in the next life to come? Thus, reincarnation, even if it *were* true, would be nothing but a series of unending failures.

Enough of the "religious" options; let's briefly explore a few of the ridiculous ideas floating around out there. Speaking of floating around, some people think we become ghosts after we die. This line of thinking claims that if we die "before our time," we become ghosts and aimlessly roam the earth. Not true. But try to name just *one* person in human history who died "on time." Wouldn't it stand to reason that *every* person would want at least one more day (or hour or minute) of life? If so, then we would all become ghosts. Hey, I was a fan of *Ghostbusters* when I was a kid, but I think it's time we yank the life support system on this "half-in, half-out" idea.

No, we don't become angels, either. If Jesus didn't sprout wings after His resurrection, neither will we. And I'm not even going to get started on zombies. . . .

When we study what the Bible says—even at a surface level—about what happens when we die, we see that it offers only two alternatives: heaven or hell. So, now that we know

Eschatology

Eschatology is the study of the end times and the final events that will occur when the world comes to an end. It isn't restricted to what happens when we die; eschatology also tries to get a handle on everything related to the end times, including the return of Christ, His judgment, the destiny of every human who's ever lived, and much more. Of course, this side of eternity, we cannot know everything about the end-of-time eternity because there are questions the Bible simply doesn't answer. But, God's Word does tell us all we need to know about spending our eternity with Him or apart from Him, and that alone makes eschatology worth the effort.

there are only two ways to go, let's discuss both of them in greater detail, beginning with hell.

Hell: A Terrible End to a Terrible Journey

Forgive me, but I'm going to assume that you got your ideas and information about hell from an episode of *South Park*, or from a comic strip, or from reading Dante's *Inferno*. If so, your concept of hell probably revolves around the devil—fully equipped with horns, pitchfork, and a pointy tail—torturing people (people we don't like or who are different from us, of course) in a place that's engulfed in flames.

Let's take a look at what the Bible says.

Many of the Bible's writers addressed the subject of hell; no one should be surprised that the apostle Paul was one of them, given everything he wrote about. In 2 Thessalonians 1:6, Paul encouraged his fellow believers by declaring to them that "God is just," and that "trouble" awaits those who make trouble for His people. Then Paul described the punishment that Jesus would inflict on them:

He [Jesus] will punish those who do not know
God and do not obey the gospel of our Lord
Jesus. They will be punished with everlasting
destruction and shut out from the presence of the
Lord and from the glory of his might.
(2 Thessalonians 1:8–9)

The book of Revelation, written by the apostle John, the only disciple of Jesus who did not die for his faith, has much to say about hell. In fact, as apocalyptic literature, and as the last book of the Bible, Revelation has a lot to say about how *all* end-time events will play out in history. In Revelation 14:10–11, John wrote about what will happen to people who follow the cleverly disguised tricks of the devil:

They, too, will drink the wine of God's fury, which
has been poured full strength into the cup of his
wrath. They will be tormented with burning sulfur
in the presence of the holy angels and of the Lamb
[Jesus]. And the smoke of their torment will rise
for ever and ever. There will be no rest day or night
for those who worship the beast [Satan's minion]
and its image, or for anyone who receives the mark
of its name.

Then, toward the end of the book, John described the final judgment of all humanity:

The devil, who deceived them, was thrown into the lake of burning sulfur, where the beast and the false prophet had been thrown. They will be tormented day and night for ever and ever. Then I saw a great white throne and him [Jesus] who was seated on it. The earth and the heavens fled from his presence, and there was no place for them. And I saw the dead, great and small, standing before the throne, and books were opened. Another book was opened, which is the book of life. The dead were judged according to what they had done as recorded in the books. The sea gave up the dead that were in it, and death and Hades gave up the dead that were in them, and each person was judged according to what they had done. Then death and Hades were thrown into the lake of fire. The lake of fire is the second death. Anyone whose name was not found written in the book of life was thrown into the lake of fire. (Revelation 20:10–15)

Everlasting destruction. Lake of fire. God's fury. Torment. That's how the Bible describes hell. To be clear, hell sounds much worse than Minnesota in January. But where did Paul and John get their descriptions of hell?

Evidently from Jesus Himself.

In Matthew 13:49–50, Jesus said that *"the angels will come and separate the wicked from the righteous and throw them into the blazing furnace, where there will be weeping and gnashing of teeth.*" Later in Matthew's Gospel, Jesus described hell as "*the eternal fire*" (v. 25:41). In Mark's Gospel, Jesus describes hell as the place where "*the fire never goes out*" and "*the fire is not quenched*" (vs. 9:43, 48). And in one of Jesus' most graphic teachings, Luke 16:19–31, He described hell as a tormenting, agonizing fire. (We'll look at this story in greater detail in the session at the end of this chapter.)

Most people probably can't hear Jesus' description of hell and not squirm in their seats. . .*at least a little.* We have a hard time connecting Jesus, who is infinitely good, with hell, which is unfathomably bad, because our culture has concocted a "nice-guy-only" image of Jesus that is devoid of the justice and judgment He promised throughout His teachings. (And those sissy churches aren't doing anything to correct this erroneous idea.) It's as if we want to do Jesus a favor and distance Him from the idea of such a place, but separating the two is more difficult than most would imagine.

According to literary genius Dorothy Sayers, it's actually *impossible.*

Sayers, an English-born novelist, poet, playwright, essayist, and translator knew about literature. During Sayers's lifetime, many thinkers pondered the reality of hell and questioned the origin of the heavily disputed doctrine. Though plenty of her contemporaries traced the idea of hell to the Dark Ages, Sayers applied her literary talents to a study of the Bible and came up with a much different source altogether:

> *There seems to be a kind of conspiracy, especially among middle-aged writers of vaguely liberal tendency, to forget, or to conceal, where the doctrine of hell comes from. One finds frequent references to the "cruel and abominable medieval doctrine of Hell," or "the childish and grotesque medieval imagery of physical fire and worms". . . .*
>
> *But the case is quite otherwise; let us face the facts. The doctrine of hell is not "medieval": it is Christ's. It is not a device of "medieval priestcraft" for frightening people into giving money to the church: it is Christ's deliberate judgment on sin. . . . We cannot repudiate Hell without altogether repudiating Christ.*[7]

Hell sounds awful, but the most terrifying aspect of it may be its duration. The Bible says it lasts forever, or *eternally*. There's no easy way to grasp the length of eternity; it casts a long shadow over us and our petty life spans. If you can, imagine a rope that's a million miles long—*yes, a million miles long!* Now imagine laying one slender hair from your head perpendicular across the middle of the rope.

You're still not even close to representing your (woefully short) life span against the backdrop of eternity.

You see, the rope that's a million miles long is *only* a million miles long. Eternity will not last for one million years, or two million years, or eighty-six million years. Eternity thunders past billions. . .and trillions. Eternity means eternity. That's how long hell lasts.

There's a lot of talk these days—*and some of it by pastors*—about judgment, eternity, and hell. Some teach that God's judgment is temporary, that His wrath against humanity's sin can be lessened after a certain amount of time has passed. Some argue that people who are separated from God in hell will one day be "paroled" right into heaven.

Let me be perfectly clear: nowhere is this taught in God's words. Hell isn't a life sentence. It's an eternal sentence.

At this point, it's natural to ask if the concept of "eternal punishment" is even consistent with the loving God found in the Bible. If God is so good and hell is so bad, why would He send people there?

Simple. He doesn't.

Now that doesn't mean there aren't people in hell. It just means that God didn't *send* them there. (Likewise, God doesn't *send* anyone to heaven, either.) God simply honors our lifelong decisions about His perfect Son, Jesus.

Like salvation, heaven and hell hinge on Jesus; where we spend eternity depends solely on what we've done with Jesus. If we reject His offer of salvation from our sins and are bent on living apart from God on earth, God honors that decision by allowing us to continue to live apart from Him. . .for all eternity. *"Look, I know you didn't want to spend any of your eighty-one years on earth with Me, but now you're stuck with Me for the rest of eternity. Take that!"* That's not God. He isn't going to force Himself on us. So, let's dispense with the notion that God arbitrarily sends some people to hell and not others. Nothing could be further from the truth. (Conversely, if we've dedicated our earthly lives to following Jesus, God invites us to simply continue our relationship with Him in heaven, face-to-face. But let's not get ahead of ourselves.)

Let me highlight one often overlooked fact about hell that usually brings tremendous encouragement: *Hell wasn't created for us in the first place.* In Matthew 25, Jesus gives a description of His final judgment on humanity, which will happen at the end of time. He uses the illustration of a shepherd separating sheep from goats. He praises the "sheep" on His right, but then condemns the "goats" on His left.

> *"Then he will say to those on his left, 'Depart from me, you who are cursed, into the eternal fire prepared for the devil and his angels." (Matthew 25:41)*

Did you catch that? God prepared "the eternal fire" for "the devil and his angels." God didn't create hell for humans. He created hell to punish the enemy who came between us and Him. To be honest, I put hell in the same category as maximum security prisons. Both are necessary, but I'm not going to either one. Prisons exist for lawbreakers. . .not pastors who come to complete stops at intersections and pay their taxes on time. Hell exists for the devil, his angels, and those who are bent on living their lives apart from God's perfect and life-changing love.

Even the greatest biblical scholars admit there's much

we don't know about hell. After all, nobody's ever gone there and posted pics on Instagram. But for those who have even a *shallow* understanding of Scripture's truth, that limited amount of information isn't so troubling. After all, what's the point of knowing every single finite detail about a place you have no intention of ever visiting?

The most confident statement that can be made about hell is this: *It's a terrible ending to a terrible journey*. A person goes to hell because he or she lived life apart from Jesus. No matter how much wealth, fame, and influence a person amasses in this life, if he or she lived apart from Jesus, life wasn't what it could have been or should have been. And when that regrettable journey comes to an end in hell, it is a terrible ending to a terrible journey.

And to think that a joyous and wonderful alternative exists, and people don't choose it.

Heaven: Forever Home

Perhaps the best way to describe heaven is by contrasting it with hell. Though hell was not created for us, heaven was. In his world-famous book *Mere Christianity*, C. S. Lewis, famed author of the Chronicles of Narnia, wrote this about heaven:

> *If I find in myself a desire which no experience*
> *in this world can satisfy, the most probable*
> *explanation is that I was made for another world.*
> *If none of my earthly pleasures satisfy it, that does*
> *not prove that the universe is a fraud. Probably*

earthly pleasures were never meant to satisfy it,
but only to arouse it, to suggest the real thing. If
that is so, I must take care, on the one hand, never
to despise, or to be unthankful for, these earthly
blessings, and on the other, never to mistake them
for the something else of which they are only a
kind of copy, or echo, or mirage. I must keep alive
in myself the desire for my true country, which I
shall not find till after death.[8]

That's heaven. The home we were made for.

So much could be said about heaven—infinitely more than about hell—simply because God is there. I know of no better description for heaven than "the place where God is." The absolute best part of heaven is Him. At this point in our journey, we must live by faith, because we cannot see God. But one day we will see Him face-to-face. Everything else about heaven is less important than this first reality, but let's take a quick look at what heaven will be like by turning again to the best authority on heaven, God's words.

If we consult the book of Revelation again, we find that the apostle John turned his pen to a fascinating description of heaven.

Then I saw "a new heaven and a new earth," for
the first heaven and the first earth had passed
away, and there was no longer any sea. I saw
the Holy City, the new Jerusalem, coming down

out of heaven from God, prepared as a bride
beautifully dressed for her husband. And I heard
a loud voice from the throne saying, "Look! God's
dwelling place is now among the people, and he
will dwell with them. They will be his people, and
God himself will be with them and be their God.
He will wipe every tear from their eyes. There will
be no more death or mourning or crying or pain,
for the old order of things has passed away."
He who was seated on the throne said, "I am
making everything new!" Then he said, "Write
this down, for these words are trustworthy and
true." (Revelation 21:1–5)

Anyone who is married—or has at least been to a wedding—
has some understanding of the beauty John tries to convey
in this passage. He uses the imagery of a bride "beautifully
dressed" on the day of her wedding to capture the splendor,
glory, and majesty of the place called "God's dwelling place."
John not only tells us that God is there, he also goes to great
lengths to tell us what's *not* there.

Heaven isn't a place of tears; God personally wipes them
from our eyes. Heaven isn't a place of death or mourning or
crying or pain; those things have come to an end. Each of
those obstacles had their run on earth; but in heaven, God
makes everything new and perfect. With broad strokes, John
said *"the old order of things has passed away."*

The apostle Paul weighed in on heaven by describing it

as...umm...a bit indescribable.

> For now we see only a reflection as in a mirror;
> then we shall see face to face. Now I know in part;
> then I shall know fully, even as I am fully known.
> (1 Corinthians 13:12)

Without a doubt, this hope brought comfort to Paul's heart. When he wrote those words two thousand years ago, there were things he simply didn't know about heaven. But when he arrived and saw Jesus face-to-face, his questions were answered and his wonderings were satisfied.

The same is true for all who go to heaven!

On this side of eternity, there are things we just won't know about heaven. *What will our bodies look like. . .and what will we wear? Will we recognize one another? Can we see those who are still on earth? Do all dogs really go to heaven? And what will we do all day for an eternity?*

Answering most of the questions about heaven involves at least a little speculation. I won't do that here; that's what YouTube preachers are for. I'm content with the knowledge that I will see Jesus face-to-face, worship simultaneously with millions of others (many of whom don't speak my language), reconnect with loved ones who arrived before me, and hang out with the likes of Moses, Gideon, Daniel, Ruth, Paul, Peter, and a guy named Habakkuk. *(I really hope I pronounce his name correctly when I speak to him!)* Think about how cool it will be to hear Moses describe (firsthand) what it looked like when the Red Sea split in two; or listen to David talk about the shock on everyone's faces when he killed Goliath with just one stone; or hear Daniel reminisce about spending the night in a den of overgrown kitties.

Those are my people. And I am theirs.

Perhaps that's what defines *home* more than anything else. Home isn't a bed, a backyard, or an address; home is where our loved ones are. The Gospel has taken me to every corner of the United States and to countries around the globe, as well. I have friends in multiple time zones, but home is the one place on earth where I am *fully* known and *unconditionally* loved. No matter how long the trip or how far I travel, I know when I'm home. Though we've never been there or seen it, and though we cannot even imagine it, heaven will be instantly recognizable to us, because it is our true home. In fact, it is the home that Jesus said He was building for us.

> *"Do not let your hearts be troubled. You believe in God; believe also in me. My Father's house has many rooms; if that were not so, would I have told you that I am going there to prepare a place for you? And if I go and prepare a place for you, I will come back and take you to be with me that you also may be where I am." (John 14:1–3)*

Jesus has built a home for us, and He's coming back for us so we can be with Him forever. When Dorothy in *The Wizard of Oz* says, "There's no place like home," she has no idea how right she is.

The Biggest Decision in Life. . .and the Afterlife

Neither heaven nor hell can be completely described in one book, let alone both places in *one chapter* of one book. But we aren't trying to describe the indescribable in this chapter; we are trying to answer the ultimate question: *What happens when we die?*

The answer is simple: *we decide.*

We get to choose where we will spend eternity, because eternity is based on Jesus. If we choose Jesus, we've chosen heaven. If we don't choose Jesus, we've chosen hell. That's because heaven and hell hinge on our relationship (or lack of relationship) with Jesus. Granted, millions of people—if not *billions* of people—believe that heaven and hell hinge on human behavior. They believe that heaven is for "good" people and hell is for "bad" people. That belief is utterly and unequivocally wrong. The Bible teaches from beginning to end that we are *all* bad people because of our sin nature. *No one* is good.

That reality is precisely why our decision about Jesus is so important. The decision we make about Jesus completely dictates where we spend eternity. What we do with Jesus determines everything in life. . .*and in the life to come.*

Talk about a big decision. . . .

Make no mistake; heaven is exclusive. The only ones invited to go there are those who've been rescued from their sins by Jesus so they can live their lives for His glory and not their own. Some think this exclusivity is unfair. . .yet those very people manage their homes in the exact same manner that

God manages His. Think about it. Doesn't everyone have rules for who *can* and *cannot* enter their home? Then why can't God? Heaven is His idea and His creation. He welcomes everyone who responds appropriately to His invitation through Jesus.

Heaven and hell are both a reality, and we will go to one of them based on what we decided about Jesus. That's what the Bible says will happen when we die.

God's words can be trusted in this life...and in the life to come.

Session 7

Heaven and Hell

What happens when we die?

Big Idea: We all die. The only time to prepare for the afterlife is in *this* life.

Passage: Luke 16:19–31

Discussion Starter: *A Date with Death*

An old tale from the Middle East speaks of a merchant from Baghdad who sent his servant to the market one day. Before long, the servant came back, white as a ghost and trembling with fear.

In great anxiety, he said to his master, "Down in the market I was jostled by a woman in the crowd, and when I turned around, I saw it was Death who had jostled me. She looked at me and made a threatening gesture. Master, please lend me your horse, for I must hasten away to avoid her! I will ride to Samarra and there I will hide. Death will not find me there."

Wanting to be helpful, the merchant loaned him his horse,

and the servant galloped away in great haste. Later the merchant went down to the marketplace and saw Death standing in the crowd. He went over to her and asked, "Why did you frighten my servant this morning? Why did you make a threatening gesture?"

"That was not a threatening gesture," Death said. "It was only a start of surprise. I was astonished to see him in Baghdad, for I have an appointment with him tonight in Samarra."

According to the Bible, everyone has "an appointment in Samarra," so to speak. With such high stakes, the most important question to answer is this: *Are you prepared for yours?*

Opening Questions

1. In the story, the servant was clearly afraid of dying. Do you think most people fear death? Why or why not?

2. Even though the servant failed, he took great pains to try to cheat his appointment with death. What are some real world ways in which people try (and fail) to cheat their appointment with death?

3. If you were given the opportunity to learn the exact time and cause of your death, would you choose to know it? Why or why not?

4. Are most people adequately prepared for death? How do you know?

Bible Passage
Luke 16:19–31

*There was a rich man who was dressed in purple and fine linen and lived in luxury every day.
At his gate was laid a beggar named Lazarus, covered with sores and longing to eat what fell from the rich man's table. Even the dogs came and licked his sores.*

The time came when the beggar died and the angels carried him to Abraham's side. The rich man also died and was buried. In Hades, where he was in torment, he looked up and saw Abraham far away, with Lazarus by his side. So he called to him, "Father Abraham, have pity on me and send Lazarus to dip the tip of his finger in water and cool my tongue, because I am in agony in this fire."

But Abraham replied, "Son, remember that in your lifetime you received your good things, while Lazarus received bad things, but now he is comforted here and you are in agony. And besides all this, between us and you a great chasm has been set in place, so that those who want to go from here to you cannot, nor can anyone cross over from there to us."

He answered, "Then I beg you, father, send Lazarus to my family, for I have five brothers. Let him warn them, so that they will not also come to this place of torment."

> *Abraham replied, "They have Moses and the Prophets; let them listen to them."*
>
> *"No, father Abraham," he said, "but if someone from the dead goes to them, they will repent."*
>
> *He said to him, "If they do not listen to Moses and the Prophets, they will not be convinced even if someone rises from the dead."*

Study Questions

1. How are the eternities of the two men described in the passage?

2. If you could see either an actual photo of heaven *or* an actual photo of hell, which would you choose to see? Why?

3. What "big idea" was Jesus trying to teach us in the passage about Lazarus and the rich man? How do you know?

4. According to this story, repentance plays a huge role in determining our final destination. What is repentance, and how does it help reinforce the idea that "heaven and hell hinge on Jesus"?

5. In Jesus' story, Abraham says that the rich man's family wouldn't repent even if someone were to rise from the dead. How did he know that? (Remember, Jesus would later die and rise from the dead.)

Deeper Questions

1. In Matthew 19:23–24, Jesus said, *"Truly I tell you, it is hard for someone who is rich to enter the kingdom of heaven. Again I tell you, it is easier for a camel to go through the eye of a needle than for someone who is rich to enter the kingdom of God."* True to His word, in the passage above, it was, in fact, the rich man who went to hell. Is it really more difficult for a rich person to enter heaven? If so, why?

2. Take a look at R. H. Savage's quote about his struggle to believe in hell (http:// itslikethis.org/?p=1405). Why do so many people wrestle with the idea of eternal punishment (when they don't wrestle with the idea of eternal peace and joy)?

3. Take a look at the prison reduction program that was botched by a computer glitch (http://itslikethis.org/?p=2311). What does this story reveal about the differences between human judgment/justice and God's judgment/justice?

Application Questions

1. Knowing that death is a reality for *all* of us, what have you done to prepare for it? What, if anything, do you still need to do?

2. You probably have friends, family members, or loved ones who aren't prepared for death and eternity. What will you do to help them prepare for their life after death?

Final Word

I have a friend who says, "Thousands of people will die today who've never died before." It's his comical/cynical way of admitting that death is a reality for every person. It really is true; one-out-of-one people die these days. Nobody's getting out of here alive. In fact, God's words even tell us this in Hebrews 9:27: *"People are destined to die once, and after that to face judgment."*

As I type these lines, I'm at a restaurant in central Florida, en route to a friend's funeral. Orville, whose name should tell you which generation he hails from, died a few days ago, and the services are in his hometown later this afternoon. I met Orville during the last year of his life, and during the time I knew him he was largely confined to a wheelchair—and later, to the bed in which he eventually died.

I visited Orville every Monday morning at a nursing home and we talked about matters of faith, family, and the inevitable future. With every passing month, his body became weaker and his voice fainter. But Orville didn't face death with any fear or uncertainty. As a fellow Floridian, Orville knew that death and judgment were like hurricanes; you don't dodge them, you simply prepare for them.

And that's exactly what he did.

Decades before I was born, Orville repented of his sins and put his entire trust in Jesus because he knew that heaven and hell hinged on Him. Then Orville spent the remainder of his days living for the glory of Jesus Christ. Right now, Orville is hanging out with Jesus and that former beggar named Lazarus.

The servant from Baghdad; the rich man and Lazarus; Orville. Some were prepared to face death. . .*and some were not.* All of them have stepped into eternity and all of them could tell us the importance of preparing for the afterlife in *this* life.

There are only two options. Heaven offers an end to all sorrow and suffering in an eternity spent face-to-face with God. Hell is a place of indescribable torment designed for those who rebel against God and reject His Son, who came to forgive them of their sin. One of the two destinations awaits each of us. We get to decide.

Choose wisely. Choose today.

8

Discipleship

Can Christianity (really) change my life?

There are several things in life that can deeply change you. If you experience them, you're going to be a different person. End of story.

For example, touching an electric fence will, without question, change a person's life. It changes a person's level of respect for scientific terms such as *volts, watts, ohms. . .and groans*. It also tends to change a person's friends—especially those who were responsible for issuing the challenge in the first place.

Bottom line: you'll be a different person after touching an electric fence.

Getting married also changes a person. . .especially if that person happens to be a man. At the wedding, he lays out a string of promises, ending with "till death do us part," and then he actually has to keep them. . .for the rest of his life! Then there's the whole *sharing* thing: the bedcovers, the last slice of pizza, and of course the TV remote. The breaking point for any man, regardless of how strong he may be, is somewhere around the seventy-second episode of *America's Next Top Model*.

Marriage just has a way of changing you.

Becoming a parent changes you, as well. For starters, it changed where my wife and I stored the permanent markers. *Rookie mistake*. Having a son also changed what I eat. I remember the good ol' days when I got to eat *all* of my own french fries. . . . Not anymore! If you want to eat all your own fries in my family, keep one eye open during prayer. Just sayin'. Becoming a parent also changed the frequency with which I cry. Once upon a time, I was a manly man who cried only when a piano fell on me or a crocodile bit off a limb. Nowadays I become a blubbering pool of tears and snot when my son asks if he can sit in my lap (while we watch Star Wars Episode 6 for the ninety-fourth time).

Becoming a parent *changes* you. On every level.

Life is filled with these kinds of experiences. Some of them are awesome; some of them are traumatic. But they all have in common that they change us in some way. We are different because of them, and we can never be the same again.

Following Jesus. . .Step-by-Step

Meeting Jesus can certainly be a life-changing experience. When we come to know Jesus as the God who died on the cross to forgive our sin, our lives should be different. . .and that difference should be obvious. In fact, that difference should be so great that when others look at us, they actually see a completely new person.

But that only happens if we follow Jesus.

Looking at the New Testament Gospels, it seems as if Jesus' favorite line was "*Follow me.*" He said it to Peter and Andrew while they were fishing (Mark 1:17). He said it to Matthew while the tax collector was counting his money (Matthew 9:9). Jesus said it to Philip (John 1:43), and even to a wealthy ruler (Luke 18:22). Jesus even said it to Peter a second time (John 21:19).

When Jesus said, "Follow me," He was essentially inviting others to live like Him. That means He wanted them to go where He went, say what He said, love who He loved (everyone!), and do what He did. Of course, He also wanted them to avoid what He avoided, namely, sin. He wants the exact same for us. This is *discipleship* in its most basic form.

If we live like Jesus, it's absolutely impossible not to be deeply changed. When we live like Jesus, we become completely different people and we get to live completely new lives. Following Jesus allows us to say, "That's who I *was*. This is who I *am*."

Admittedly, this chapter is where the rubber meets the

Discipleship

Understanding discipleship is simple; accomplishing it is much more difficult. Discipleship is simply the act of following Jesus. He is the teacher/leader and we are the disciples/followers. When we become Jesus' disciples, we are essentially trying to live like He does. In Mark 8:34, Jesus outlines the obligations of discipleship, "He called the crowd to him along with his disciples and said: 'Whoever wants to be my disciple must deny themselves and take up their cross and follow me." Following Jesus may cost you a lot, but not following Jesus will cost you everything.

road. It's where faith (Christianity) meets real life. This is the make-or-break moment for Jesus and His teachings. Does His way work, or is it just another empty philosophy?

We won't know the answer to that all-important question unless we know what He taught and put it into practice for ourselves. So let's take a closer look at what Jesus said and did to see if it really leads to new life.

Here's what it takes to follow Jesus, step-by-step.

Step 1: Stop Sinning

Yeah, I know. This may sound like a no-brainer to *you*, but years of ministry have introduced me to lots and lots of people who don't understand the importance of leaving their sin behind them when they begin to follow Jesus.

It's as if they somehow forgot that Jesus came to rescue them from their sin.

From cover to cover, God's words denounce sin and teach us to abandon any and all sinful practices. The most poignant example comes from John 8:1–11. In this passage, Jesus' enemies brought a woman to Him who was caught *in the very act* of adultery, with the hopes of trapping Jesus in His words. The stakes were high for Jesus, and the woman, too; her sin was a capital offense in those days. But Jesus' answer turned the tables on the woman's accusers, and He shamed them so badly that they all walked away in silence. After all the bad guys were gone, Jesus looked at the embarrassed woman whose life He had just saved and gave her a simple but life-changing command: *"Go now and leave your life of sin."*

In other words, Jesus told her, "Stop sinning!" Jesus' command applies to each of us today. We cannot go with Him if we don't stop sinning. Jesus never sinned, mainly because He was God and He knew the devastating consequences of sin. When Jesus said "stop sinning," that's exactly what He meant. Jesus wants our sinning to come to a *complete* stop. "Slowing down" won't cut it.

Think about it like this: the obese guy who weighs 417 pounds doesn't need to *reduce* his intake of Dunkin' Donuts. He needs to *stop* his intake. . .*immediately* and *completely*! Likewise, the woman who constantly gossips about others doesn't need to "cut back" on her verbal defamation; she needs to "cut it out." *Entirely!*

Let's say you just found out that your new neighbor is a serial killer. His rate of homicide hovers somewhere around one vicious slaying per week. Knowing this, would you ask him to reduce his frequency to one brutal killing per month? Per year? *Per decade?* No! You'd want that psycho to put down the machete for good!

Or how about the husband who's been having a string of extramarital affairs behind his wife's back. Suppose he "finds Jesus" one day and confesses to her, "Honey, I've been living a sinful life. But from now on, I'm gonna cheat on you a whole lot less. You have my word."

That guy better sleep with one eye open.

Stealing. Lying. Drunkenness. Envy. No matter what sort of sin we've grown accustomed to, Jesus wants us to stop it. *Completely.* He knows it's the only way to have a truly new life.

But that's just the first step we must take.

Step 2: Study God's Words

We already addressed the tremendous importance of studying God's words back in chapter 2, but the significance of this step bears repeating here.

The Bible, God's words, is the main way He communicates with us. Therefore, we need to study it faithfully; Jesus did. Throughout the Gospels, Jesus quoted the Old Testament time and time again. Given that He was a Jewish rabbi—*and God*—He would have had the entire Old Testament memorized. (The New Testament didn't exist yet; it would be written during the next sixty or so years.)

Not only did Jesus possess an excellent understanding of God's words, He expected others to have a strong understanding of them, as well. That's evident from the number of times Jesus asked people what *they'd* read from God's words. Take a look at just a *few* examples from Matthew's Gospel:

- *"Haven't you read," he [Jesus] replied, "that at the beginning the Creator 'made them male and female. . .?" (v. 19:4)*

- *"Have you never read, 'From the lips of children and infants you have ordained praise'?" (v. 21:16)*

- *"Have you never read in the Scriptures: 'The stone the builders rejected has become the cornerstone;*

the Lord has done this, and it is marvelous in our
eyes'?" (v. 21:42)

- *"Have you not read what God said to you, 'I am*
  the God of Abraham, the God of Isaac, and the
  God of Jacob'? He is not the God of the dead but of
  the living." (vs. 22:31–32)

Jesus summed up how important God's words are when the devil tempted Him at the beginning of His ministry. In Matthew 4:4, Jesus once again appealed to the Old Testament:

"It is written: 'Man shall not live on bread alone, but
on every word that comes from the mouth of God.'"

God's words sustain our very lives. So don't just *read* the Bible from time to time; *study* it *daily*. It will outline God's plan for your new life.

Step 3: Pray Expectantly

Nothing goes better with Bible study than prayer. Since prayer is our only way of speaking with God, we should do it all day long. In fact, one of the shortest verses in the Bible, 1 Thessalonians 5:17, offers a mere two words of instruction that can change our lives: *"Pray continually."* That simple command outlines one of the most important steps we can take toward new life.

Prayer needs to be important to us because of how

important it was to Jesus. Reading through the Gospels reveals that Jesus did a lot of praying. He prayed alone (Matthew 14:23) and with others (John 11:41–42). He prayed before big decisions (Luke 6:12) and in moments of unimaginable stress (Matthew 26:36). He prayed for Himself, His disciples, and *you* (John 17:1–26). For Jesus, prayer was crucial.

Sadly, many Christians have reduced prayer to a few canned phrases they say at specific points throughout their day— over a meal or at bedtime, perhaps—without much fervor or anticipation. Those are not the kinds of prayers we find in the Bible. The prayers recorded in Scripture were prayed by men and women, in the midst of life-and-death circumstances, who knew that unless God acted, unless God did what only God could do, grave consequences would follow. Having the power of God active in their lives was the highest priority for them, so they prayed with great expectation.

The most influential Christians throughout church history have done the same. They constantly told God that everything depended on Him. . .because it did. For example, George Müller, a nineteenth-century Christian living in England, built orphanages and schools that affected the lives of thousands of impoverished children. He accomplished everything without ever asking people for money (or going into debt). He was able to do so because he wouldn't start a single day without spending several hours in prayer asking God to miraculously meet the needs of his life-changing facilities.

Hudson Taylor adopted the same prayer-dependent strategy for his world-famous mission to China. Early in his walk with Jesus, Taylor experimented with the power of prayer until he was confident he could build an intercontinental mission on God's provision. He did, and that same mission agency still exists today. After all this time, Taylor's legacy of prayer is an example for all of us.

Martin Luther, the man who kicked off the Protestant Reformation, devoted three hours to prayer every day. He said Christians should pray as naturally as a shoemaker makes shoes and as naturally as a tailor makes a coat. Jonathan Edwards, the preacher who had a significant role in the Great Awakening, wrote about the "sweet hours" spent on the banks of the Hudson River, "rapt and swallowed up in God."

These people were simply praying the way Jesus instructed them to pray. In His very first sermon, Jesus outlined how we should pray:

> *"This, then, is how you should pray: 'Our Father in heaven, hallowed be your name, your kingdom come, your will be done, on earth as it is in heaven. Give us today our daily bread, and forgive us our debts, as we also have forgiven our debtors. And lead us not into temptation, but deliver us from the evil one.'" (Matthew 6:9–13)*

A lot of churches pray these very words in their worship services, but that misses the point. Jesus didn't say "Pray this," He said "Pray *like* this." In other words, we are to use this prayer as a template or model when we pray. If we break down Jesus' prayer line by line and apply His teaching to our lives, not only will we spend much more time in prayer, we'll also see many more results.

Continual and expectant prayer leads to new life like nothing else.

Step 4: Give Generously

You were waiting for it, right? How can any pastor write a book and not mention money? All right, all right, simmer down. I'm not going to take up an offering. . .but we're going to talk about money because of how important *you* think it is.

Many people think that God is little more than a celestial loan shark looking to get rich off the backs of His underlings. But here's the deal: God is *already* rich. In Psalm 50:10, Asaph wrote that "the cattle on a thousand hills" belong to God. In fact, God is so loaded that He considers one of our most prized possessions, gold, as worthless as asphalt. The description of heaven in Revelation 21 tells us that much of the city is made of gold, including the streets.

Yeah, that's how God rolls.

I'm going to make the issue of giving very, very simple. God doesn't command us to give because *He* needs it; He commands us to give because *we* need it. There's no better way for us to learn how to trust God than to give as He commands us to give. In Matthew 10:8, Jesus commanded His disciples to give freely because they had freely received. Further, Jesus taught about the importance of giving (Matthew 22:21), commended those who gave (Mark 12:41–44), and modeled giving Himself (Matthew 17:24–25).

Malachi 3:8–10 tells us how seriously God takes the idea of giving:

> *"Will a mere mortal rob God? Yet you rob me.*
> *"But you ask, 'How are we robbing you?'*
> *"In tithes and offerings. You are under a*
> *curse—your whole nation—because you are*
> *robbing me. Bring the whole tithe into the*
> *storehouse, that there may be food in my house.*
> *Test me in this," says the LORD Almighty, "and see*
> *if I will not throw open the floodgates of heaven*
> *and pour out so much blessing that there will not*
> *be room enough to store it."*

Look, as a pastor, I cannot recommend stealing from anyone. But whatever you do, don't steal from the matchless God who created the universe. That's just not a very smart move.

If you've never made giving a part of your life, here's my humble suggestion. Start by giving *frequently*. Get in the practice of giving on a regular basis. Nothing builds discipline like repetition. But as soon as you can, transition into giving *proportionately*. The Bible's word for this is *tithing*, and the standard is 10 percent of your income. But don't misunderstand; this is just the baseline, the absolute minimum that's required. If you commit to giving like this, I guarantee you'll do more with 90 percent and God's blessing than you can with 100 percent and no blessing. But don't stop there, either. Mature disciples understand the need to give *generously*. When God sent Jesus to die for our sins, it was a tremendous sacrifice for Him. When we mirror His example in giving, we become more like Him.

Looking more like Him is the whole purpose of new life.

Step 5: Worship Corporately

Chapter 6 focused on why attending church is important, but like the reminder to study the Bible, it bears repeating. When we participate in worship on a regular basis, with others, we are following Jesus' example. Granted, Jesus never attended the type of church services we have today, because they didn't exist until much later, but He spent a lot of His time at the temple and in synagogues, places where God was worshipped during those times.

We humans have a bad habit of putting ourselves at the center of the universe; worship corrects our perspective in life. Worship allows us to respond to God, and it's best done the same way prayer is done: *with expectation*. When we assemble for worship, we should anticipate that God will reveal Himself and transform us. That's the whole point.

But worshipping God alongside others is beneficial for us in other ways, as well. When we spend time together in worship on a regular basis, strengthening one another's faith, we can face the challenges of life more effectively. Like our physical bodies, the church is more than the sum of its parts. We are stronger together than we can ever be alone.

I do a lot of grilling. My favorite animal is a dead one that

I can cook over a pile of white-hot charcoal. I start by stacking the briquettes in the shape of a pyramid, dousing them in lighter fluid, striking a match, and then tossing on the steaks while sipping on an ice-cold root beer.

Occasionally, the intense heat causes the pyramid to shift, and a briquette (or two) will fall off the flaming pile of charcoal. No matter how hot those briquettes are, if they stay isolated from the larger fire, they will inevitably lose their flame. That's how our fellowship is within the church. When we allow ourselves to be separated from one another, we tend to lose our fire for God.

But here's the good news: if that stray charcoal briquette is placed back on the pile of flaming coals, it will regain its flame. The same is true for us; we can be strengthened by rejoining the godly relationships available to us. So, if you've gotten out of the habit of worshipping with others on a regular basis, search for a great church that allows you to connect with God and serve Him.

The fellowship we experience in Christ is not a perk; it's a foundational necessity! The Christian life was never designed to be lived in isolation. We need to do life *together*.

Together life leads to *new* life.

Step 6: Serve Selflessly

No one knows more about serving others than Jesus. He spent time teaching people so they would know the truth, and He healed many of them, as well. He even washed the feet of His disciples one evening, a task so menial that it was typically reserved for the lowest of servants in those days. But His most endearing act of service was dying on the cross for the payment of our sins. Serving others was a major part of Jesus' ministry. In fact, in Mark 10:42–45, Jesus said that serving others is one of the reasons that He came to earth.

> *Jesus called [the disciples] together and said, "You know that those who are regarded as rulers of the Gentiles lord it over them, and their high officials exercise authority over them. Not so with you. Instead, whoever wants to become great among you must be your servant, and whoever wants to be first must be slave of all. For even the Son of Man did not come to be served, but to serve, and to give his life as a ransom for many."*

God came to serve humans, and when He did, He left a life-changing mark on us. If we serve others as selflessly as Jesus did, we can do the same.

Max Kolbe did.

Father Maximilian Kolbe was a Polish-born priest who affected the lives of thousands around the world through a ministry he founded within the Roman Catholic Church. But his real legacy centers on a selfless act of service for one man named Francis. . .at a place called Auschwitz.

In February 1941, the occupying German forces in Poland shut down the monastery where Father Kolbe lived. He was arrested and later carted off to Auschwitz, the Holocaust's most notorious death camp. There the middle-aged priest helped his fellow prisoners by preaching the Gospel, serving Communion, and offering them encouragement on a daily basis. (He did all this in addition to the strenuous manual labor and severe beatings inflicted on him.) The harsh treatment landed him in one sick ward after another. But in every way, Father Kolbe led by sacrificial example. He offered his portions of food and drink to fellow prisoners and made sure the doctors cared for others before treating him.

Kolbe's situation was slowly improving when he received word that a prisoner from his barracks was thought to have escaped from the camp (though he was later found dead in the camp latrine). At Auschwitz, one escapee meant ten prisoners would die.

Commandant Karl Fritsch, the camp deputy, personally selected the condemned men. One by one, he randomly pointed at prisoners until the grim quota had been met. Only human, those not selected for execution were relieved.

But Sergeant Francis Gajowniczek had been selected.

The soldier's wails for his wife and children he'd leave behind reached the ears of Kolbe, prompting the priest to one last act of selfless service. Walking over to the guard, Kolbe said, "I am a Catholic priest. I would like to take his place because he has a wife and children." The uncanny selflessness startled the commanding officer for a moment, but he waved his hand in compliance and said, "Away."

That word sealed the fate of Father Maximilian Kolbe.

He and the other nine condemned prisoners were marched to an underground cell and stripped of their clothes. Subjected to execution by starvation, the men languished in the basement bunker until hunger or disease took their lives. Three weeks later, only Father Kolbe and three others remained. Needing to free up the cell for newly condemned prisoners, the Nazis gave the four remaining prisoners lethal injections of carbolic acid.

In August 1941, in a place where death seemed to reign unchecked, one man gave life to another through a selfless act of sacrifice.

We can do the same if we're willing to serve others the way Jesus served.

Step 7: Witness Passionately

A person's last words usually give an indication of what was important to him or her. For example, John Adams was totally focused on outliving his political rival Thomas Jefferson. While lying on his deathbed, he used his final breath to gasp, "Thomas Jefferson. . .still survives." Ironically, Jefferson had died a few hours earlier on that same day, July 4, 1826.

In 1555, as Hugh Latimer and Nicholas Ridley were about to be burned at the stake for preaching about Jesus, Bishop Latimer turned to his friend and said, "Be of good comfort Master Ridley, and play the man. We shall this day light such a candle, by God's grace, in England, as I trust shall never be put out." Those men had committed their lives to spreading the Gospel of Jesus, and it showed, right down to their final words.

Contrary to some people's thinking, Jesus' last words on earth were not uttered on the cross. Yes, He did say, "It is finished," just before He died, but *after* His resurrection, He again spoke to His disciples:

> *Then Jesus came to them [the Eleven] and said, "All authority in heaven and on earth has been given to me. Therefore go and make disciples of all nations, baptizing them in the name of the Father and of the Son and of the Holy Spirit, and teaching them to obey everything I have commanded you. And surely I am with you always, to the very end of the age."(Matthew 28:18–20)*

Jesus could have used His last moments on Earth (before ascending into heaven) talking about the importance of Bible studies, church attendance, or even prayer. But He didn't. With great calculation, He used His final words to say, "Go everywhere and tell everybody everything about Me." And He is depending on us to do that.

Bible scholars—and other devoted Christians—call that passage from Matthew the Great Commission. Sadly, millions of lackluster believers live as if it's nothing more than the Good Suggestion.

Not Joseph.

Joseph was a proud Masai warrior living in eastern Africa when he first heard the Gospel of Jesus Christ on the side of a hot, dusty road. In that moment, he dedicated his life to Christ and immediately made plans to share the same Good News with members of his tribe.

But this warrior had never been in a fight like the one he was about to walk into.

In his village, Joseph went from hut to hut, telling everyone about the cross of Jesus and the salvation it offered. He expected them to eagerly embrace Christ as he had, but to his amazement, the people not only rejected the Gospel, they became violent in their opposition. The men of the village seized him and held him to the ground while the women beat him with strands of barbed wire. Afterward, he was dragged from the village and left to die alone in the wild.

Joseph managed to crawl to a watering hole, and there, after several days of passing in and out of consciousness, he finally regained his strength. He was perplexed by the hostile reception he'd received from people he'd known all his life. He decided he must have left something out or told the story of Jesus incorrectly. So after rehearsing his important message over and over, he went back to share his faith again.

Joseph limped into the circle of huts and began to proclaim Jesus' love. "He died for you, so that you might have forgiveness and come to know the living God!" he cried. Again, he was flung to the ground by the men of the village while the women beat him; wounds that had just begun to heal were reopened. Like the first time, they dragged his unconscious body away from the village and left him to die.

To have survived the first beating was truly remarkable. To live through the second one was borderline miraculous. But several days later, Joseph awoke in the wilderness, bruised and scarred.

And determined to go back yet again.

Joseph returned to the small village, but this time they attacked him before he even had a chance to open his mouth. While they flogged him the third time, Joseph pleaded with them to seek the forgiveness of Jesus Christ. The last thing he saw before passing out was the women weeping as they beat him.

When he regained consciousness the third time, it was in his own bed. The men and women who had so severely beaten him were now trying to save his life and nurse him back to health. Noticing that Joseph thought his message was important enough to repeatedly risk his life, the villagers eagerly listened to him share the Gospel, and many of them put their trust in Christ.

All that because one guy took Jesus' command seriously.

We cannot live a new life with Jesus if we don't do what He commands.

The Requirements of New Life

Millions of people, ranging from seekers to skeptics, wonder if Christianity can really change a person's life. Let me answer that question as simply as I can.

No, Christianity can't change you.

Christianity couldn't change Peter. It couldn't change Paul or Matthew or John or Barnabas. . .or anybody else mentioned in the Bible. Christianity couldn't change Martin Luther, John Wesley, or Billy Graham, either.

Only Jesus can change us.

David R. Smith

You see, God's purpose is not for us to be Christians, but to be Christlike. (Sadly, there is a difference.) We know what God wants because His words tell us. In Genesis 1:26, God verbalized His wildest intention in all of creation: *"Let us make mankind in our image, in our likeness."* Of course, we ruined that image—*His image*—with our sin, so God sent Jesus to rescue us and totally transform us so that we might once again look like Him. In fact, Romans 8:29 claims that God wants us to *"be conformed to the image of his Son."*

Transformation

To understand the concept of transformation, think about Optimus Prime, the leader of the Autobots in the Transformers movie franchise. One moment he's a semi-truck barreling down the highway, and then he transforms into a towering robot ready to defeat the Decepticons. What does a semi-truck have in common with a robot? That's right; absolutely nothing. But what does a caterpillar have in common with a butterfly? Transformation is when one thing becomes something else entirely. God wants our old life of sin to be transformed (through Jesus) to a new life in Him.

No set of rules can change us. No philosophy can change us. No religion can change us. Only Jesus, the Savior of the world, can change us.

But it's gonna take some discipline on our part.

I've learned a lot about discipline in the past four years. Until four years ago, my policy on running was simple: *I didn't.* Of course, I made exceptions if a big dog was chasing me or the ice cream truck driver didn't see me coming. But four years ago, my neighbor got me into running. *(As a consequence, I no longer speak to that neighbor.)* Now I go running. On purpose.

234

With absolutely zero ice cream involved.

And I'll have you know that I run like a gazelle. *A fat, wounded, asthmatic, gazelle.*

But I keep running, nonetheless. One step after the other. Every day. Oftentimes, it's a torturous affair. I tell myself, "Just one more street. Just one more mailbox. Just one more step."

That's how it is with following Jesus; we do it one step at a time.

Throughout this chapter, we looked at some important steps we can take to follow Jesus. There are certainly others, as well—such as solitude (getting alone with God), meditation (reflection for the soul), Scripture memorization. . .and everybody's favorite, fasting (skipping a meal to intentionally spend time with God). Regardless of the steps we take, the key is that we keep on taking them. Over and over and over again.

One step never completes a journey. Neither will one step lead to new life. New life takes time. *Lots of it.*

Anyone telling you otherwise is selling something.

It takes time to lose weight, doesn't it? An overweight person who wants a new life can't just diet for one day and be ready for the cover of a magazine. Likewise, it takes time for a woman to give birth to new life. . .about nine months to be exact. New life doesn't just happen. The journey to new life is made up of many, many steps. Following Jesus isn't a sprint; it's more like a marathon. . .a marathon that lasts the rest of our lives.

Disciplining ourselves for new life won't always be easy, but it will always be worth it.

Keep following the one who chased after you.

Session 8

Discipleship

Can Christianity (really) change my life?

Big Idea: When we follow Jesus, our lives must be different, and that difference must be obvious.

Passage: Luke 19:1–10

Discussion Starter: *Brittni Turns to Jesus*

Brittni Ruiz was an eighteen-year-old college student when she was first approached by men who spoke of her beauty and a bright future in "romance movies." Lured by the promise of fame and money, she traveled to Los Angeles the very next day and filmed her first scene.

Little did Brittni know how much that day would affect the next seven years of her life.

The impressionable young girl began a career in adult entertainment that spanned from 2005 to 2012 and included almost three hundred adult films. Now known as Jenna Presley, the "World's Hottest Porn Star," she was compelled to work for weeks on end without any breaks, shooting two to three scenes per day, engaging in regrettable sexual acts with one complete stranger after another. It was a chaotic time to say the least.

And the chaos took its toll. . .as it always does.

Her petite frame could barely endure the physical punishment inflicted on it by the demands of the porn industry. Jenna admitted to becoming closed off, and she described herself as "a rubber Barbie doll" who was "emotionless, empty, plastic, and hopeless." She desperately wanted to leave the industry but, like so many other young women, felt trapped in guilt, regret, and shame.

In order to cope with the pace and the pain of porn, Jenna turned to drugs, alcohol, and self-injury. At several low points, she even attempted suicide.

However, there was one source of light in Jenna's life: the team from XXXChurch. Led by pastor Craig Gross, this California-based ministry helps those in the porn industry and those addicted to its product. They routinely attend the adult expos held around the world and share Jesus with the men and women working in the adult entertainment business, handing out Bibles, T-shirts, and hugs. Seeing Jenna's struggles, they continually sought her out and offered her much-needed friendship and encouragement.

The long talks with members of XXXChurch's team eventually took root in Jenna's heart. When she finally realized that fame and money could no longer satisfy her, she made one more turn, this time to Jesus. In late 2012, she gave her life to Christ at a church she visited with her grandparents. It was a radical conversion, to say the least.

Since then, she's returned to the porn conventions—as Brittni Ruiz, not Jenna Presley—with the message of hope she found in Jesus, and Jesus alone. She has already helped some of her former coworkers discover Jesus and escape the life of porn. One changed life is leading to another changed life.

Which is exactly what Jesus intended all along.

Opening Questions

1. How would you describe Brittni *before* she met Jesus and *after* she met Him? What were some of the differences?

2. Brittni is now using her new life to reach others trapped in the porn industry. Why do you think she does this?

3. Without a doubt, Jesus totally transformed Brittni's life and is using her in mighty ways to reach others with His life-changing love. It's nothing short of a radical conversion. Does this describe most other people's conversions? Why or why not?

4. Do you know someone who had a conversion similar to Brittni's? In other words, do you know

somebody who met Jesus and had his or her life totally changed? If so, explain.

5. If you are following Jesus, what are some of the ways your life has been changed?

Bible Passage

Luke 19:1–10

Zacchaeus, the man we're about to meet, worked as a tax collector. In Jesus' day, tax collectors gathered money from their Jewish neighbors and gave it to the hated Romans, who had conquered Israel in a war fought years earlier. Consequently, most Jews thought tax collecting was little more than treason. Making matters worse, tax collectors often took *more* money than was due and simply pocketed the surplus. Thus, not only were tax collectors helping the Romans, they were also stealing from their fellow Jews. Bottom line: Zacchaeus would have been the most unpopular person in Jericho. But Jesus wanted to talk with him anyway.

> *Jesus entered Jericho and was passing through. A man was there by the name of Zacchaeus; he was a chief tax collector and was wealthy. He wanted to see who Jesus was, but because he was short he could not see over the crowd. So he ran ahead and climbed a sycamore-fig tree to see him, since Jesus was coming that way.*
>
> *When Jesus reached the spot, he looked up and*

*said to him, "Zacchaeus, come down immediately.
I must stay at your house today." So he came down
at once and welcomed him gladly.*

*All the people saw this and began to mutter,
"He has gone to be the guest of a sinner."*

*But Zacchaeus stood up and said to the Lord,
"Look, Lord! Here and now I give half of my
possessions to the poor, and if I have cheated anybody
out of anything, I will pay back four times the
amount."*

*Jesus said to him, "Today salvation has come
to this house, because this man, too, is a son of
Abraham. For the Son of Man came to seek and to
save the lost."*

Study Questions

1. How does Luke describe Zacchaeus? Which descriptor is the most significant, in your opinion?

2. Luke tells us that the people "began to mutter" when Jesus went to Zacchaeus's house. Why was that?

3. How was Zacchaeus's life changed after he met Jesus? How do you know?

4. What does it say about Jesus that He was willing to befriend an open and hated sinner?

Deeper Questions

1. Which of the seven steps to following Jesus discussed in this chapter (stop sinning, study God's words, pray expectantly, give generously, worship corporately, serve selflessly, witness passionately) is hardest for you? Why?

2. Read the conversion account of the apostle Paul in Acts 26:1–23. It includes Luke's description of Paul's life before meeting Jesus, how he met Jesus, and how his life was different as a result of meeting Jesus. Based on Paul's story, Zacchaeus's story, and Brittni's story, how would you describe the change Jesus expects to see in you?

3. Take a look at the humorous cartoon on the It's Like This website about a man trying to change (http://itslikethis.org/?p=4259). Why do so many people only pretend to change instead of actually changing?

Application Questions

1. If your friends and family members were asked how Christlike you are, what would they say?

2. What are some ways your life needs to change so you look more like Jesus?

3. What will that require of you? Are you willing to do it?

Final Word

Hernando Cortez was an all-in *sort of guy.*

Before he turned thirty, the young Spaniard had become very successful in politics and war. His zeal and his willingness to take risks quickly established him as a man of influence in the newly discovered West Indies. By the summer of 1519, Cortez had set his sights on a brand-new target: Mexico.

Against his governor's orders, Cortez gathered a few horses and cannons, about five hundred men, and a fleet of eleven ships, and hastily set sail for a land he believed to be laden with gold.

As soon as he set foot on the beaches of Mexico, Cortez realized how desperate his situation was. Ahead of him lay Montezuma and his fierce Aztec warriors; behind him would soon be another fleet of Spanish Conquistadors sent by the superior whose orders he disobeyed.

Cortez knew what he had to do, and he didn't waste a moment getting started. As soon as his men and supplies were off the boats and safely ashore, Cortez ordered every ship to be run aground in the shallow waters near the beach.

The ships that had brought them to Mexico and were supposed to take them back home had now been completely destroyed. Cortez took such a bold risk because he knew that the boats provided his men with a mental "safety net" of retreat. Though no Conquistador would dare say it, many believed that if the fighting became too rough, they could always retreat to the boats and return to Cuba.

Not anymore.

In one of the boldest gambles in military history, Cortez deliberately cut off *any* possibility of retreat. There would be *no* turning back.

Jesus was an *all-in* sort of guy, too. He proved that by dying on the cross to rescue us from our sin. *It doesn't get more all-in than that.* When we follow Jesus, He expects that *we* will be all-in like He is. As King of kings and Lord of lords, Jesus has every right to expect our full allegiance. If we follow Jesus, there can be no turning back.

Take a few moments to read through the following questions. They are simple yes or no questions, but answering them honestly will help you gauge your level of commitment to Jesus. Since you began following Jesus:

1.   Have you truly abandoned your sinful ways?
2.   Have you made amends for the pain you've caused?
3.   Are His desires truly first in your life?
4.   Have your entertainment choices changed?
5.   Do you spend time reading God's words listening to Him?
6.   Do you love others as much as you love yourself?
7.   Do you give generously so others can hear of His life-changing love?

There's zero room for mediocrity in discipleship. When we follow Jesus, our lives must be different and that difference must be obvious.

Regardless of where you are on the journey, keep following. Every step with Jesus leads to new life.

Endnotes

1. Victor Searcher, *The Farewell to Lincoln* (New York: Abingdon, 1965), 126–127.

2. *United States v. Wilson*, 32 U.S. 161 (1833).

3. Aislinn Laing, "Swimmer Savaged by Shark Saved by Two Good Samaritans," *The Telegraph*, September 29, 2011; www.telegraph.co.uk/news/worldnews/africaandindianocean/southafrica/8797151/Swimmer-savaged-by-shark-saved-by-two-good-Samaritans.html.

4. "Statistics Don't Tell the Whole Story When It Comes to Church Attendance," ChurchLeaders.com; www.churchleaders.com/pastors/pastor-articles/170739-statistics-don-t-tell-the-whole-story-when-it-comes-to-church-attendance.html.

5. "Letter to Ezra Stiles," recounted in John Bigelow, *The Works of Benjamin Franklin* (New York: Putnam, 1904.)

6. "Americans Describe Their Views about Life after Death," Barna Group, October 21, 2003; www.barna.org/barna-update/article/5-barna-update/128-americans-describe-their-views-about-life-after-death#.VAowLvldV8E.

7. Dorothy Sayers, *A Matter of Eternity*, ed. Rosamond Kent Sprague (Grand Rapids: Eerdmans, 1973), 86.

8. C. S. Lewis, *Mere Christianity* (New York: HarperCollins, 1952), 137–138.

About the Author

Even though he's earned two undergraduate degrees and one advanced degree, David R. Smith prefers to have simple conversations about faith and life. He pastors First Baptist Church in Linden, Florida, where he lives with his wife, Jenn, and their son, Josiah. When he's not preaching, he's usually looking for great barbecue joints or his errant golf shots.